Travel Guide To

Ocho Rios, JAMAICA

Escape to Narbonne:
The Must-Have Travel Companion
for Your Adventure!

Wybikes Hinton

COPYRIGHT NOTICE

This publication is copyright protected. This is only for personal use. No part of this publication may be, including but not limited to, reproduced, in any form or medium, stored in a data retrieval system or transmitted by or through any means, without prior written permission from the Author / Publisher.

Legal action will be pursued if this is breached.

DISCLAIMER

Please note that the information contained within this document is for educational purposes only. The information contained herein has been obtained from sources believed to be reliable at the time of publication. The opinions expressed herein are subject to change without notice.

Readers acknowledge that the Author / Publisher is not engaging in rendering legal, financial or professional advice. The Publisher / Author disclaims all warranties as to the accuracy, completeness, or adequacy of such information.

The Publisher assumes no liability for errors, omissions, or inadequacies in the information contained herein or from the interpretations thereof. The publisher / Author specifically disclaims any liability from the use or application of the information contained herein or from the interpretations thereof.

TABLE OF CONTENT

Copyright Notice ii
Disclaimer iii
Table of Content iv
INTRODUCTION 10
Welcome To OCHO RIOS! 10
   About This Travel Guide. 10
   Why Ocho Rios? 11
   How To Use This Guide. 11

Chapter 1 14
Introduction to Ocho Rios. 14
   Overview of Ocho Rios. 14
   Historical Background 15
   Geography and Climate. 16

Chapter 2 18
Planning Your Trip to Ocho Rios. 18
   Best Time To Visit 18
   Visa and Entry Requirements. 20
   Transport Options 22

Chapter 3 24
Accommodation Options in Ocho Rios. 24
   Overview of Accommodation Options. 24

Luxury resorts 26

    Budget-Friendly Hotels 28

    Boutique Guesthouses. 31

    Unique Stays... 33

    Top Recommended Accommodation 36

    Selecting the Suitable Accommodation for You.................... 38

    Bookkeeping Tips & Tricks 41

Chapter 4 45
Exploring Ocho Rios Beaches 45

    Major Beaches in Ocho Rios 45

    Water Sport and Activities... 47

    Beach Safety Tips. 50

Chapter 5 54
Must-see Attractions in Ocho Rios.. 54

    Dunn's River Falls 54

    Mystic Mountain 56

    Dolphin Cove... 58

Chapter 6 61
Cultural Experiences in Ocho Rios. 61

    Local Markets and Craft Stores 61

    Jamaican Cuisine and Dining Experience 63

    Reggae Music and Dance Culture. 65

Chapter 7 68
Outdoor Adventures in Ocho Rios.. 68

    Rainforest Hiking Trails 68

    Zipline and Canopy Tours 70

Safari Excursions with ATVs and Jeeps 71

Chapter 8 74
Exploring Ocho Rios' Waterfalls. 74
- Blue Hole. 74
- Konoko Falls. 76
- Reach Falls. 78

Chapter 9 81
Family-friendly Activities in Ocho Rios 81
- Turtle River Park. 81
- Horseback Riding Tours. 83
- Family-Friendly Beaches. 85

Chapter 10 87
Nightlife & Entertainment in Ocho Rios. 87
- Bars and Nightclubs 87
- Live Music Venues. 89
- Cultural Performances. 91

Chapter 11 94
Shopping in Ocho Rios. 94
- Ocho Rios Craft Market. 94
- Shopping Malls and Plazas. 96
- Local Souvenirs & Gifts 98

Chapter 12 101
Day Trips & Excursions From Ocho Rios 101
- Kingston Day Trip. 101
- Blue Mountain Excursion 103

Port Antonio Tour 105

Chapter 13 108
Wellness & Spa Retreats in Ocho Rios. 108

Spa Resorts and Wellness Centres 108

Holistic Healing Practices. 110

Yoga and Meditation Retreats. 113

Chapter 14 117
Itinerary and Sample Plans 117

Weekend Getaway 117

Cultural Immersion 121

Outdoor Adventure 124

Family-friendly trip. 128

Budget Travel 131

Solo Traveler's Guide 134

Romantic Getaways in Ocho Rios. 138

Chapter 15 144
Local Festivals and Events in Ocho Rios 144

Ocho Rios Jazz Festival 144

Bob Marley's Birthday Celebration 146

Reggae Sumfest. 147

Chapter 16 149
Photography and Sightseeing Tips. 149

Top Photography Spots in Ocho Rios 149

Embracing The Essence of Jamaican Culture 151

Photo Etiquette and Respectful Practices 153

Chapter 17 156
Safety and Travel Tips. 156
Health and Safety Precautions. 156

Emergency Contacts and Services. 158

Responsible Travel Practices 159

Chapter 18 161
Budget-Friendly Travel Tips. 161
Ways to Save Money in Ocho Rios 161

Affordable Dining Options 163

Free or Low-cost Activities 164

Chapter 19 168
Cultural Etiquette and Customs 168
Jamaican Greetings And Social Norms. 168

Understanding Rastafari Culture 170

Respect of Local Traditions and Customs 172

Chapter 20 175
Sustainable Tourism Initiatives in Ocho Rios. 175
Environmentally Friendly Accommodations 175

Conservation Efforts. 178

Community Engagement Projects 180

Chapter 21 184
Planning Special Events in Ocho Rios 184
Destination Weddings 184

Honeymoon Packages 187

Anniversary Celebration 189

- Chapter 22 192
- Conclusions and Final Tips 192
  - Summary of Ocho Rios Highlights 192
  - Final Recommendation for Visitors 194
  - Inspirational Stories and Testimonials. 196
- APPENDIX 198
- Useful resources 198
  - Emergency Contacts: 198
  - Maps and Navigational Tools. 199
  - Additional Reading and References 200
  - Useful Local Phrases: 201
  - Addresses and Locations for Popular Accommodations 201
  - Addresses and locations of popular restaurants and cafes. . 202
  - Addresses And Locations Of Popular Bars And Clubs. 203
  - Addresses And Locations Of The Top Attractions 204
  - Map of Ocho Rios, Jamaica 206
  - Map of Restaurants 207
  - Map of Things to Do in Ocho Rios 208
  - Map of Museums 209

INTRODUCTION

WELCOME TO OCHO RIOS!

Welcome to Ocho Rios, a bustling beach town on Jamaica's northern coastlines. Ocho Rios, with its beautiful beaches, thick jungles, and rich cultural legacy, entices guests looking for adventure, relaxation, and amazing experiences.

About This Travel Guide.

So, you intend to visit Ocho Rios? Congratulations for picking one of the most stunning Caribbean places! This travel book is the ideal companion, helping you make the most of your time in Ocho Rios. This guide is your road map to a wonderful Jamaican journey, with insider ideas on where to stay and what to visit, as well as practical guidance on safety and cultural etiquette.

Why Ocho Rios?

"Why Ocho Rios?" you could ask. Okay, let me paint a picture for you. Consider cascading waterfalls that plunge into turquoise pools, palm-fringed beaches lapped by crystal-clear seas, and green hillsides cloaked in mist. That's Ocho Rios in a nutshell: a gorgeous paradise that embodies Jamaica's natural beauty.

But Ocho Rios is more than just an attractive face. It's a paradise for outdoor enthusiasts, with activities like as zip-lining under the rainforest canopy, snorkeling amid vibrant coral reefs, and hiking to secret waterfalls. It's also a cultural melting pot where you can eat traditional Jamaican food, dance to reggae music, and immerse yourself in the island's thriving arts community.

Aside from its natural and cultural charms, Ocho Rios has a warm and friendly vibe that is uniquely Jamaican. The inhabitants, noted for their warm welcome and contagious smiles, will make you feel right at home the moment you arrive. So why Ocho Rios? Because it is a location that satisfies the senses, refreshes the soul, and leaves you wanting more.

How To Use This Guide.

Now that you're ready to start your Ocho Rios journey, let's talk about how to get the most out of this book.

Navigate Easily: This guide is divided into chapters and subtopics for simple access. Whether you're looking for lodging alternatives, organizing outdoor adventures, or getting insider information on local events, simply flip through the chapters to discover what you need.

Insider Insights: This guide contains insider tips and advice from seasoned visitors and locals alike. These pearls of knowledge can help you discover hidden jewels, avoid tourist traps, and enjoy Ocho Rios like a genuine insider.

Customize Your Experience: Ocho Rios has something for everyone, whether you're traveling alone, with family, or in a group. Use this advice to create an itinerary depending on your interests, budget, and travel style. Whether you want adventure, leisure, or cultural immersion, Ocho Rios offers it all.

Stay Informed and Safe: While Ocho Rios is typically a safe and inviting place, it's crucial to be aware of local customs, safety precautions, and travel warnings. This book contains critical information to help you traverse unknown terrain and have a safe and enjoyable journey.

Embrace the Journey: Above all, remember that travel is more than merely checking off bucket-list items. It's all about enjoying the adventure, engaging with other cultures, and making lasting experiences. So, while you discover the beauties of Ocho Rios, be prepared for unexpected experiences, cherish every moment, and let the spirit of Jamaica to capture your heart.

With this guide on your side, you're set for a memorable adventure across Ocho Rios' stunning scenery and colorful culture. So, pack your bags, brush off your spirit of adventure, and prepare to be swept away by the charm of Jamaica's gem of the north coast. Adventure awaits!

Chapter 1

INTRODUCTION TO OCHO RIOS.

Ocho Rios, a bustling seaside town on Jamaica's northern coast, entices visitors with magnificent natural beauty, a rich history, and genuine friendliness.

In this chapter, we will look at the essence of Ocho Rios, including an overview of its attractions, historical roots, and distinctive topography and climate.

Overview of Ocho Rios.

Ocho Rios, which translates to "Eight Rivers," is a thriving tourist town in the parish of Saint Ann, Jamaica. Despite its name, Ocho Rios does not contain eight rivers, but is named for the eight rivers that previously ran through the area. Today, Ocho Rios is well-known for its beautiful beaches, lush scenery, and active culture, making it a popular destination for those seeking both rest and adventure.

One of Ocho Rios' biggest appeals is its breathtaking natural beauty, which includes gushing waterfalls, gorgeous beaches, and thick jungles. From the spectacular Dunn's River Falls to the peaceful Blue Hole, Ocho Rios offers a plethora of outdoor activities for both nature lovers and thrill seekers.

In addition to its natural beauty, Ocho Rios is rich in Jamaican culture and history. Visitors may tour ancient plantations, eat real Jamaican food, and immerse themselves in the island's lively music culture. Ocho Rios provides a genuinely immersive immersion into Jamaican culture, with vibrant markets, colorful festivals, and friendly residents.

Historical Background.

Ocho Rios' history is connected with Jamaica's intricate fabric, which has been molded by indigenous peoples, European colonization, and African ancestry. Prior to European arrival, the Taino people lived in the region, taking use of the island's rich grounds and bountiful resources.

With Christopher Columbus' arrival in 1494, Jamaica became a key center for European exploration and colonization. The Spanish developed colonies and plantations throughout the island, using its natural riches and local labor force. However, Spanish dominion was short-lived; in 1655, the British invaded Jamaica, ushering in a new period of colonialism.

During the colonial time, Ocho Rios became a hub of trade and business, with a bustling port for the export of sugar, rum, and other items. The town's strategic location made it a target for pirate attacks and naval conflicts, which contributed to its colorful history and marine legend.

Ocho Rios had substantial expansion during the twentieth century, as tourism established as a vital business in Jamaica. The development of hotels, resorts, and tourist attractions converted Ocho Rios into a top destination for visitors from all over the world, establishing its status as the "Jewel of Jamaica's North Coast."

Today, Ocho Rios is a thriving cultural and commercial hub where the echoes of the past blend with the rhythms of modern life. From ancient sites to modern attractions, Ocho Rios provides an intriguing peek into Jamaica's rich historical and cultural legacy.

Geography and Climate.

Ocho Rios is endowed with a magnificent location, wedged between the lush hills of Jamaica's interior and the dazzling Caribbean Sea. The town's coastline position provides a gorgeous backdrop of blue seas and palm-fringed beaches, making it a picture-perfect destination for beachgoers and sunbathers.

The geology of Ocho Rios is distinguished by its diversified terrain, which includes sandy beaches, craggy cliffs, and lush rainforests. The hamlet is surrounded by rich tropical vegetation, including towering palm trees, blooming orchids, and exotic plants.

Ocho Rios has a tropical environment, with mild temperatures and plenty of sunshine throughout the year. The average temperature is approximately 80°F (27°C), making it an excellent choice for year-round vacation. Visitors should be prepared for periodic rain showers, particularly during the rainy season, which runs from May to October.

Despite the rare downpour, rain showers are often short and give a pleasant relief from the heat. The rainy season provides lush foliage and blossoming flowers, which enhances the town's natural beauty and charm.

Chapter 2

PLANNING YOUR TRIP TO OCHO RIOS.

Planning a trip to Ocho Rios is an exciting undertaking, full of anticipation for the activities that await.

In this chapter, we'll walk you through the most important parts of trip preparation, such as determining the ideal time to visit, comprehending visa requirements, and examining transportation alternatives to and from this wonderful country.

Best Time To Visit

The ideal time to visit Ocho Rios is primarily determined by your weather choices, crowd size, and price. Ocho Rios has a warm and tropical environment all year, but there are some times of year when it is very beneficial for visitors.

Peak Season (December to April): The peak season in Ocho Rios corresponds with the dry season, which lasts from

December to April. The weather is mainly sunny and dry, with temperatures ranging from the mid-70s to low 80s Fahrenheit (24-29°C). The peak season also corresponds with the winter holidays and spring break, making it the most popular time of year for tourism in Ocho Rios. Accommodation costs tend to be greater, and famous sites may be busier. However, if you prefer vivid atmospheres and bright sky, the peak season is the best time to come.

Shoulder Season (May and November): The months of May and November provide a combination of pleasant weather and less crowds. While there may be periodic rain showers, particularly in May, the shoulder seasons let you to experience Ocho Rios' attractions without the high season crowds. Furthermore, housing and airline may be less expensive during certain months, making it a cost-effective alternative for tourists.

Off-peak Season (June to October): Ocho Rios' off-peak season is during the rainy season, which extends from June to October. While rainfall may be more common at this season, it is usually in the form of brief, strong showers followed by clear sky. Off-peak season offers the lowest costs for lodging and flights, making it an appealing alternative for budget visitors. Furthermore, the lush foliage and blossoming flowers that arise from the rain might enhance the town's natural charm.

Finally, the optimum time to visit Ocho Rios is determined by your preferred weather, budget, and crowd levels. When organizing your vacation, keep your top priorities in mind to guarantee a memorable and pleasurable experience.

Visa and Entry Requirements.

Before you travel to Ocho Rios, be sure you understand Jamaica's visa and entrance procedures. The particular criteria may differ based on your nationality and the reason for your stay.

Visa Exemptions: Citizens of certain countries may be excluded from acquiring a visa for short-term travels to Jamaica. These exemptions generally apply to passengers from the Caribbean Community (CARICOM) and a number of other nations, including the United States, Canada, the United Kingdom, and European Union member states. However, the length of stay permitted under visa exemptions might vary, therefore it is essential to examine the exact rules for your nationality.

Visa Requirements: If you are going from a nation that requires a visa to enter Jamaica, you must apply for one before your trip. Visa requirements may involve filling out an application form, submitting proof of adequate cash for your stay, and showing a valid passport with at least six months' validity beyond the desired stay. It is best to apply for your visa far ahead of your travel dates to allow for processing time.

Entry Formalities: Upon arriving in Jamaica, visitors must pass through immigration and customs checks. You will need to bring your passport, completed immigration documents, and any necessary visas or entrance permits. Immigration officers may also inquire about the purpose of your visit and the length of your stay. It is critical to answer these questions accurately and adhere to any extra entrance criteria imposed by immigration officials.

COVID-19 Entry conditions: In response to the COVID-19 epidemic, Jamaica has imposed additional entry conditions for visitors. These procedures may include submitting documentation of a negative COVID-19 test done within a certain duration before arrival, filling out a travel authorization form, and following health and safety regulations upon admission. When planning a vacation to Ocho Rios, it is critical to remain up to speed on the most recent travel warnings and entrance requirements for COVID-19.

You may speed the admission procedure and start your Ocho Rios experience on the right foot by being acquainted with Jamaica's visa and entry requirements, as well as ensuring that you have the relevant papers.

Transport Options

Getting to and from Ocho Rios is reasonably simple, with a number of transportation choices available to meet any traveler's requirements and interests.

Air Travel: The nearest international airport to Ocho Rios is Sangster International Airport (MBJ) in Montego Bay, about 90 minutes away by car. Sangster International Airport is Jamaica's busiest airport, serving as a gateway for tourists arriving from all over the world. Visitors to Ocho Rios can reach the city via shuttle bus, private transport, or rental vehicle from the airport.

Ground Transportation: Once in Ocho Rios, there are numerous ways to move around town and see the surrounding surroundings. Rental automobiles are accessible at both the airport and in Ocho Rios, enabling flexibility and convenience for independent tourists. Furthermore, taxis and private automobile services are commonly accessible and may be booked through hotels or summoned on the street.

Public transit: Ocho Rios has a public transit system that includes buses and route taxis known as "coasters." Buses and coasters go on fixed routes around the town and nearby areas, making them a cheap way to get about. However, public transit schedules may be less frequent in outlying places, so plan your travel appropriately.

Tour Operators and Excursions: There are various tour operators and excursion organizations that offer guided tours and day trips to Ocho Rios and the surrounding area. These excursions frequently include transportation, admission fees, and expert guides who may give information about the area's history, culture, and natural beauties.

Walking and Cycling: Ocho Rios is a pedestrian-friendly town with several attractions, restaurants, and stores within walking distance of one another. Exploring Ocho Rios on foot allows you to soak up the colorful ambiance while discovering hidden gems along the way. Bicycle rentals are also available for those who want to explore at their own leisure while taking in the fresh sea wind.

Using the many transportation choices available in Ocho Rios, you can easily travel the town and its surrounds, letting you to maximize your time in this tropical paradise.

To summarize, arranging a vacation to Ocho Rios needs careful consideration of the ideal time to come, knowing visa and entrance regulations, and researching transportation choices to guarantee a smooth and pleasurable journey. By planning ahead of time and being acquainted with these critical areas of trip preparation, you can set the stage for an outstanding vacation in Ocho Rios.

Chapter 3

ACCOMMODATION OPTIONS IN OCHO RIOS.

In Chapter 3, we will look at the many types of accommodations available in Ocho Rios, responding to each traveler's needs and interests. Ocho Rios has a variety of accommodations to suit every taste and budget, including luxury resorts, boutique hotels, and budget-friendly guesthouses.

Overview of Accommodation Options.

Ocho Rios has a thriving hospitality market, with a variety of lodging options ranging from opulent resorts to lovely bed & breakfasts. Whether you want an extravagant seaside getaway or a quiet refuge set in the hills, Ocho Rios has something for everyone.

Luxury Resorts: Ocho Rios is home to some of the Caribbean's most prominent luxury resorts, which provide world-class facilities, breathtaking ocean views, and exceptional service. These resorts cater to sophisticated guests looking for the utmost in comfort and leisure, offering everything from luxurious suites to private villas.

Boutique Hotels: Boutique hotels in Ocho Rios provide a more intimate and customized experience, with a distinct combination of charm, flair, and hospitality. These smaller establishments frequently have unique décor, customized service, and a peaceful ambiance, making them perfect for romantic trips or quiet retreats.

All-Inclusive Resorts: Ocho Rios is well-known for its all-inclusive resorts, which allow visitors to enjoy limitless eating, drinks, and entertainment without ever leaving the site. These resorts frequently have enormous pools, gourmet restaurants, and a wide range of activities and services to ensure a pleasant visit.

Guesthouses & Bed and Breakfasts: For guests looking for a more genuine and affordable experience, Ocho Rios' guesthouses and bed and breakfasts provide pleasant rooms and friendly service. These family-run enterprises offer a home away from home experience, with customized service and insider information on local sites and activities.

Villas and Vacation Rentals: For tourists wanting solitude and flexibility, villas and vacation rentals in Ocho Rios provide a home-like environment with all of the amenities of home. Whether you're visiting with family or friends, these large villas make an excellent base for exploring Ocho Rios at your own leisure.

Regardless of your choices or budget, Ocho Rios has a wide range of lodging alternatives to meet any traveler's needs and interests. With its breathtaking natural beauty, wonderful friendliness, and world-class amenities, Ocho Rios is the ideal location for your next vacation.

LUXURY RESORTS

Ocho Rios is synonymous with luxury, and its world-class resorts represent the pinnacle of indulgence and elegance. These luxury resorts in Ocho Rios exemplify the art of hospitality, with luxurious rooms, superb dining experiences, and unrivaled service.

Here, we'll look at seven of Ocho Rios' most well-known luxury resorts, each offering an amazing getaway to paradise.

Sandals Royal Plantation: Nestled on a secluded beach overlooking the dazzling Caribbean Sea, Sandals Royal Plantation is a luxury haven. This all-inclusive resort offers gorgeously designed apartments, excellent dining options, and premium services like butler service and private beach cabanas. Guests may engage in luxurious spa treatments, explore the vivid coral reefs, or simply rest by the pool and enjoy the sun.

Moon Palace Jamaica: Located on the beachfront of Ocho Rios, Moon Palace Jamaica combines luxury with natural beauty. The resort offers large rooms, world-class dining options, and a wide range of activities and entertainment for guests of all ages. Moon Palace Jamaica offers a variety of activities, including swimming with dolphins and teeing off on the championship golf course.

Jewel Dunn's River sand Resort & Spa: Nestled on a magnificent length of sand, Jewel Dunn's River Beach Resort & Spa is an adults-only haven of peace and relaxation. The resort offers luxury rooms, excellent dining options, and a full-service spa where visitors may enjoy revitalizing treatments and wellness activities. Jewel Dunn's River, with its quiet environment and personal service, is ideal for couples looking for a romantic break.

Couples Tower Isle: As one of Jamaica's most prominent adults-only resorts, Couples Tower Isle combines old-world charm with modern luxury. The resort's lively Caribbean atmosphere is evident in its large suites, exquisite dining selections, and diverse activities and entertainment. Couples

Tower Isle offers the ideal location for a wonderful holiday, from snorkeling in crystal-clear seas to dining on gourmet food beneath the stars.

GoldenEye: For a really unique and amazing experience, GoldenEye provides a quiet sanctuary surrounded by beautiful tropical gardens and blue oceans. This iconic resort, which was formerly home to James Bond novelist Ian Fleming, now offers sophisticated rooms, private villas, and unique facilities including a private beach and freshwater lagoon. Guests may discover the resort's rich history, savor farm-to-table cuisine, or simply relax in their own little paradise.

Luxury resorts in Ocho Rios range from isolated beachside getaways to exclusive private villas, allowing guests to relax and be sophisticated.

Budget-Friendly Hotels

Traveling on a budget does not imply compromising comfort or quality, especially when it comes to lodging in Ocho Rios. This section investigates budget-friendly hotels in Ocho Rios that provide reasonable prices without sacrificing convenience or amenities. These lodgings, ranging from modest coastal getaways to beautiful guesthouses, provide great value for budget-conscious guests.

Rooms Ocho Rios: Located in the center of Ocho Rios, Rooms Ocho Rios provides pleasant accommodation at reasonable prices. The hotel offers clean and spacious rooms, free Wi-Fi, and a convenient location near beaches, restaurants, and shopping. Guests may relax by the pool, eat real Jamaican food at the on-site restaurant, and use the hotel's tour desk to visit Ocho Rios' attractions on a budget.

Pineapple Court Hotel: Nestled in tropical grounds, the Pineapple Court Hotel provides a peaceful escape from the rush and bustle of Ocho Rios. The hotel's comfortable rooms are outfitted with modern facilities such as air conditioning, cable TV, and private balconies overlooking the gorgeous grounds. Guests may relax by the outdoor pool, eat wonderful Caribbean food in the hotel's restaurant, and take advantage of the free shuttle service to nearby sites.

Kaz Kreol Beach Lodge: Located only steps from the beach, Kaz Kreol Beach Lodge provides economical lodging with a relaxed island ambiance. The resort offers modest accommodations with ocean views, free Wi-Fi, and a laid-back attitude ideal for budget tourists. Guests may sunbathe on the private beach, eat local Jamaican food at the on-site restaurant, and visit surrounding sites including Dunn's River Falls and Mystic Mountain.

Silver Seas Hotel: Overlooking the Caribbean Sea, the Silver Seas Hotel provides affordable rooms in a fantastic beachfront position. The hotel's pleasant rooms provide ocean or garden views, air conditioning, and satellite television. Guests may unwind by the outdoor pool, dine in the hotel's restaurant, which serves Jamaican and international cuisine, and take advantage of free Wi-Fi throughout the resort.

Village Hotel Ocho Rios: Located in the center of Ocho Rios, the Village Hotel provides economical lodgings within walking distance of shopping, restaurants, and activities. The hotel offers modest but pleasant rooms, a rooftop patio with panoramic views of the town, and free Wi-Fi in public areas. Guests may explore Ocho Rios on foot, relax in the hotel's shared lounge, and take advantage of 24-hour front desk assistance.

These low-cost hotels in Ocho Rios are an ideal choice for those trying to stretch their money while maintaining comfort and convenience. With their handy locations, nice lodgings, and reasonable pricing, these hotels provide an excellent base for experiencing everything Ocho Rios has to offer without breaking the bank.

Boutique Guesthouses.

Boutique guesthouses in Ocho Rios provide a more private and customized experience, with charm, character, and a warm Jamaican welcome. These smaller facilities offer a comfortable and private ambiance, with individualized service, distinctive décor, and a sense of home away from home. Here are some of the boutique guesthouses which stand out in Ocho Rios:

Hermosa Cove - Jamaica's Villa Hotel: Nestled in a quiet cove, Hermosa Cove provides a selection of luxury villas and cottages surrounded by beautiful tropical gardens. Each villa is individually designed and decorated with local artwork and handcrafted furnishings, resulting in a tranquil and beautiful escape. Private plunge pools, outdoor showers, and fully outfitted kitchens are available to guests, along with access to a private beach, spa facilities, and gourmet eating options.

Couples Sans Souci: Located in tropical gardens overlooking the Caribbean Sea, Couples Sans Souci is an exclusive adults-only resort with old-world elegance and romance. The resort's small setting, customized service, and exquisite suites make it a favorite among couples looking for a romantic holiday. Guests may indulge in gourmet cuisine, relax by the pool, or participate in a range of activities and entertainment, such as water sports, yoga courses, and live music performances.

The Blue House Boutique Bed & Breakfast: Located in the center of Ocho Rios, The Blue House is a beautiful boutique bed and breakfast with a warm and inviting ambiance. The resort has individually furnished rooms, a lovely garden courtyard, and a public lounge where guests may unwind and mingle. Every morning, the Blue House provides a superb breakfast that includes local delicacies and fresh products from surrounding markets.

Hibiscus Lodge Hotel: Perched atop a cliff overlooking the Caribbean Sea, the Hibiscus Lodge Hotel provides panoramic views and a peaceful environment away from the rush and bustle of Ocho Rios. The hotel's large rooms and suites are elegantly designed with Caribbean-inspired furniture and include private balconies or patios that overlook the ocean or gardens. Guests may dine in the hotel's open-air restaurant, swim in the outdoor pool, or unwind on the sun terrace while admiring the stunning views.

Paradise Turtle Towers: Paradise Turtle Towers, located on the banks of the Turtle River, provides exquisite rooms in a tranquil and attractive location. The hotel's modern suites are stylishly decorated with contemporary decor and have fully outfitted kitchens, spacious living spaces, and private balconies with views of the river or ocean. Guests get access to the hotel's swimming pool, fitness center, rooftop terrace, as well as free Wi-Fi and parking.

Boutique guesthouses in Ocho Rios range from opulent villas to lovely bed & breakfasts, providing a one-of-a-kind and wonderful experience for guests wanting a more intimate and customized stay. These boutique establishments provide warm hospitality, beautiful lodgings, and attention to detail, making them ideal for a memorable holiday in Jamaica's gem of the north coast.

Unique Stays

Travelers visiting Ocho Rios may immerse themselves in distinctive and interesting lodgings that go beyond standard hotels and resorts. These unique lodgings, which range from treehouses buried in the jungle to eco-friendly lodges overlooking the Caribbean Sea, provide an exceptional experience that links tourists with Jamaica's natural beauty and cultural diversity.

 Treehouse Villas at Sandals Ochi Beach Resort: Nestled high amid the trees, the Treehouse Villas at Sandals Ochi Beach Resort provide a one-of-a-kind escape surrounded by lush tropical greenery. Each villa has lavish facilities such as private plunge pools, outdoor bathrooms, and expansive living areas with panoramic views of the resort and the ocean beyond. Guests may enjoy exclusive access to the resort's attractions, such as gourmet dining, water sports, and live entertainment, while relaxing in their private treehouse hideaway.

GoldenEye's Fleming Villa: Named after its former owner, famed novelist Ian Fleming, this historic and legendary refuge emanates charm and elegance. The villa, nestled in tropical grounds with views of the Caribbean Sea, offers exquisite rooms, private pools, and a specialized staff to meet the needs of all visitors. With its rich history and eternal attractiveness, the Fleming Villa provides an unparalleled opportunity to experience the renowned charm of GoldenEye, where Fleming wrote his famous James Bond books.

Great Huts: Nestled on the cliffs overlooking Boston Bay, Great Huts provides a rustic and eco-friendly getaway that honors Jamaica's traditional legacy and natural beauty. The site offers one-of-a-kind lodgings, such as African-style huts, treehouses, and beach cottages, each with its own particular charm and character. Guests may immerse themselves in Jamaican culture with live music, drumming sessions, and real Jamaican food provided at the on-site restaurant. With its spectacular vistas and eco-conscious attitude, Great Huts offers a really unique and rewarding experience for guests looking for a deeper connection to Jamaica.

Kanopi House: Located in the middle of the rainforest, Kanopi House provides an immersive and environmentally friendly refuge surrounded by nature's splendor. The facility offers exquisite treehouse lodgings made from locally sourced materials, complete with open-air design, panoramic views, and eco-friendly facilities. Guests may take guided treks into the neighboring rainforest, kayak along the river, or simply relax in the hammock on their private veranda while listening to the sounds of the jungle. Kanopi House, with its dedication to conservation and community empowerment, provides a one-of-a-kind chance to explore Jamaica's rainforest in an environmentally responsible atmosphere.

Firefly Beach Cottages: Set on a private stretch of beach, Firefly Beach Cottages provides a peaceful and intimate respite from the rush and bustle of Ocho Rios. The property has beautiful homes situated among lush gardens, each with spectacular views of the Caribbean Sea and direct access to a private beach. Guests may relax in hammocks, swim in the turquoise waters, or visit neighboring sights like Dunn's River Falls and Dolphin Cove. Firefly Beach Cottages offers a relaxed ambiance and customized service, making it ideal for a romantic trip or calm retreat.

These one-of-a-kind lodgings in Ocho Rios provide guests with an original and distinctive experience of the area. From luxurious treehouses to eco-friendly getaways, each resort provides a unique experience that highlights Jamaica's natural beauty, cultural legacy, and welcoming warmth.

Top Recommended Accommodation

Choosing the ideal lodging in Ocho Rios might be difficult due to the abundance of possibilities. Here are some top-rated lodgings that routinely garner wonderful ratings from guests.

Sandals Royal Plantation: Nestled on a secluded beach with views of the Caribbean Sea, Sandals Royal Plantation is one of Jamaica's top luxury resorts. This adult-only sanctuary exudes sophistication with its sumptuous suites, exquisite dining options, and unique facilities such as individual butler service and private beach cabanas. Guests may engage in luxurious spa treatments, water sports, or simply relax by the pool while taking in the tropical atmosphere. Sandals Royal Plantation raises the bar for luxury and relaxation in Ocho Rios.

Moon Palace Jamaica: With its picturesque position on the Ocho Rios shoreline, Moon Palace Jamaica perfectly combines luxury and natural beauty. The resort offers large rooms, a variety of eating options, and a wide range of activities and entertainment for guests of all ages. Whether tourists want to swim with dolphins, tee off on the golf course, or relax by the pool, Moon Palace Jamaica guarantees an unforgettable vacation. Its breathtaking ocean views and welcoming atmosphere make it an excellent choice for anyone looking for a perfect Caribbean holiday.

GoldenEye: A famous hideaway inspired by its lush surroundings, GoldenEye enchants guests with its ageless appeal and incomparable beauty. Set in tropical gardens overlooking the sea, the resort provides beautiful rooms, excellent dining experiences, and premium facilities such as private beaches and freshwater lagoons. Guests may explore the resort's rich history, participate in aquatic sports, or simply enjoy the tranquility of their villa. GoldenEye exemplifies the relaxed elegance and unique appeal of Jamaica's north coast.

Hermosa Cove - Jamaica's Villa Hotel: Nestled in a quiet cove, Hermosa Cove provides a selection of luxury villas and cottages surrounded by lush gardens. Each villa has a distinct design, private pools, and specialized staff, guaranteeing guests a perfect vacation. Hermosa Cove, with its own beach, spa amenities, and gourmet dining selections, embodies the spirit of Caribbean luxury via a combination of elegance and tranquillity.

These top suggested Ocho Rios lodgings guarantee an unforgettable visit, with each offering a unique combination of luxury, comfort, and Caribbean character. Whether you're looking for a romantic break, a family holiday, or a peaceful escape, these resorts offer the ideal setting for unique experiences in Ocho Rios.

Selecting the Suitable Accommodation for You

Choosing the correct accommodations is an important part of planning any vacation since it sets the tone for the entire experience. In Ocho Rios, a resort noted for its broad choice of lodgings, selecting the ideal place to stay necessitates careful consideration of your interests, budget, and travel style. This section gives a complete guide to navigating the process of choosing the best lodging for your Ocho Rios vacation.

Identify Your Needs and Preferences: Before you start looking for Ocho Rios accommodations, think about what you need and want. Consider your budget, location, facilities, and desired experience throughout your stay. Are you looking for a luxury seaside resort, a nice bed & breakfast, or a low-cost guesthouse? Knowing what you want can help you limit down your alternatives and simplify the decision-making process.

Determine Your Budget: When looking for lodging in Ocho Rios, it is essential to set a budget. Determine how much you are willing to pay per night, taking into account additional fees, taxes, and included facilities. Remember that Ocho Rios has a broad choice of hotel alternatives to fit any budget, from luxury resorts to low-cost guesthouses, so there's something for everyone's pocketbook.

Consider Location: The location of your accommodations might have a significant influence on your whole experience in Ocho Rios. Choose whether you want a beachfront home, a hidden getaway in the hills, or a central position among restaurants, stores, and activities. When deciding where to live, consider transit alternatives and closeness to major attractions.

Research Accommodation choices: Once you've determined your needs, preferences, and budget, you can begin looking into Ocho Rios lodging choices. Use internet travel platforms, review websites, and travel guides to look at a range of properties and read feedback from previous visitors. When assessing lodging alternatives, consider cleanliness, customer service, facilities, and overall guest happiness.

Examine facilities and Services: Take notice of the facilities and services provided by each hotel choice, and examine how they relate to your needs and preferences. Swimming pools, restaurants, wellness facilities, exercise centers, Wi-Fi access, and complementary breakfast are some of the most important things to consider. Determine which facilities are crucial for your comfort and enjoyment while in Ocho Rios.

Read Reviews and Recommendations: Feedback from previous guests can give significant insights into the quality and experience of a certain hotel. Pay attention to both good and negative evaluations to gain a complete picture of the property's strengths and drawbacks. Look for repeating themes and analyze how they could influence your decision-making.

Consider Special Offers and Packages: Keep an eye out for special offers, deals, and packages from Ocho Rios lodging providers. Many resorts and hotels provide promotions such as discounted prices, complimentary upgrades, and all-inclusive packages that combine lodging, food, activities, and other amenities. To get the most out of your stay, ask about any available specials and take advantage of them.

Contact the Accommodation Directly: If you have any particular queries or requests, please contact the accommodation directly to inquire about availability, price, and any additional accommodations you may need. Speaking with a representative can give further information and assist ensure that your requirements are satisfied throughout your stay.

Consider Your Travel Companion(s): If you're traveling with family, friends, or a significant other, think about their preferences and needs while selecting accommodations. Make sure the resort can adequately handle your group size and has amenities and services that appeal to everyone's interests and needs.

Finally, when it comes to Ocho Rios accommodations, trust your intuition. If a property seems right and matches your needs, it's probably a fantastic choice for your stay. In contrast, if anything does not seem right or meet your expectations, keep looking until you locate the ideal lodging for your Ocho Rios vacation.

Following these suggestions and taking into account your needs, interests, and budget will allow you to confidently select the best hotel for your Ocho Rios experience.

Bookkeeping Tips & Tricks

Booking accommodations is an important part of travel preparation, particularly when visiting Ocho Rios. Using clever tactics will help you acquire the greatest discounts and maximize your money. Here are some secret tips and tactics to speed up the booking process and ensure a pleasant experience:

Early Booking Advantage: It is best to book your accommodations ahead of time, especially during peak travel seasons or high-demand times like festivals or holidays. By making reservations far in advance, you not only ensure your desired dates and accommodations, but you also take advantage of early booking discounts and promotions commonly provided by hotels and resorts.

Date Flexibility: If your trip dates allow for it, be open to exploring several date ranges for the best pricing and availability. Midweek stays and off-peak seasons often have lower prices and less crowds, providing a more relaxing and cost-effective experience in Ocho Rios.

Comparison Shopping Across Platforms: Don't limit your search to just one booking site. Spend time comparing pricing on many channels, such as online travel agencies, hotel websites, and booking aggregators. Keep an eye out for exclusive bargains and discounts that may only be available on certain platforms.

Leverage Rewards Programs: Many hotel chains and booking platforms provide rewards programs that allow customers to accumulate points or receive discounts on future stays. Enroll in loyalty programs to receive member-only deals, privileges, and advantages, maximizing savings and improving your entire booking experience.

Exploring Package Deals: To save money and simplify vacation planning, consider bundling accommodations with other travel components such as flights, vehicle rentals, and activities. Numerous booking sites provide package deals and holiday packages that combine lodging with other amenities and services at discounted rates.

Hidden Fees and Surcharges: Keep in mind that there may be additional fees and surcharges that were not included in the first price quotation when choosing your accommodations. Examine the tiny print to see if taxes, resort fees, and other expenses are included, avoiding unpleasant surprises at checkout.

Flexible Cancellation Policies: Look for lodgings that provide flexible cancellation policies, especially if your trip plans are unknown or changing. Choosing hotel alternatives with forgiving cancellation policies provides peace of mind and flexibility in modifying travel arrangements as needed.

Benefits of Direct Booking: Booking directly with hotels or resorts allows you to access special benefits, upgrades, and incentives that are not available through third-party booking services. Direct booking frequently allows for direct connection with the hotel, promoting individualized support and addressing concerns swiftly.

Price Alerts and Notifications: Use the price alert capabilities given by booking platforms to keep track on swings in lodging pricing. Setting up notifications allows for quick booking when rates drop, assuring the best value for your selected stay.

Read Reviews and get suggestions: Before making your reservation, read guest reviews and get suggestions from other visitors to determine the overall quality and reputation of the property. Previous visitors' feedback provides vital insights into service quality, cleanliness, and overall client happiness.

Integrating these booking tips and techniques into your hotel selection process will allow you to confidently navigate the various alternatives in Ocho Rios, getting the appropriate housing for a memorable and gratifying vacation experience.

Chapter 4

EXPLORING OCHO RIOS BEACHES

Ocho Rios, known for its breathtaking coastline and beautiful beaches, has several possibilities for leisure, adventure, and aquatic exploration.

In this chapter, we look at the attractiveness of Ocho Rios' beaches, including the main beaches, water sports and activities, and important beach safety precautions for a memorable and pleasurable seaside experience.

Major Beaches in Ocho Rios

Ocho Rios is endowed with a variety of gorgeous beaches, each with its own distinct charm and attractiveness. Whether you're looking for pristine white sands, turquoise seas, or abundant marine life, Ocho Rios' beaches provide an exquisite refuge for both sun-seekers and water lovers.

Turtle Beach: Turtle Beach, located along the coast of Ocho Rios, captivates visitors with its smooth beaches and serene atmosphere. This lovely beach, named for the sea turtles that used to frequent its beaches, has crystal-clear waters that are great for swimming and snorkeling. Visitors may relax in the sun, explore the vivid coral reefs rich with marine life, or take a leisurely stroll along the coast.

Dunn's River Beach: Adjacent to the spectacular Dunn's River Falls, Dunn's River Beach is a popular location for nature lovers and adventurers. This lovely beach has white sand, calm waves, and spectacular views of the neighboring waterfalls. Visitors may swim in the cool waters, climb the famous falls, or simply rest and soak up the sun while observing the beautiful scenery.

Mahogany Beach: Tucked away in a hidden cove, Mahogany Beach provides a peaceful and personal atmosphere away from the throng. This hidden treasure, surrounded by lush flora and towering cliffs, offers tranquil waters excellent for swimming, kayaking, and paddleboarding. Visitors may rent lounge chairs and umbrellas, eat great Caribbean food at the oceanfront restaurant, or simply relax in the natural beauty of the area.

James Bond Beach: Immortalized in the classic James Bond film "Dr. No," oozes glamor and charm with its golden dunes and turquoise seas. This scenic beach provides a variety of water sports and activities, such as snorkeling, jet skiing, and sailing. Visitors may relax in the shade of palm palms, explore adjacent coral reefs, or take a lovely boat excursion along the shore.

Reggae Beach: Located only minutes from Ocho Rios' town core, Reggae Beach entices guests with its relaxed ambiance and energetic environment. This popular beach has white sands, swaying palm palms, and clear blue seas ideal for swimming and snorkeling. Visitors may watch live music, eat real Jamaican food at the beachside bar and grill, or participate in water activities like parasailing and banana boating.

Each of Ocho Rios' principal beaches has its own distinct ambiance and attractions, encouraging tourists to relax, explore, and make lasting experiences amidst the natural beauty of Jamaica's north coast.

Water Sport and Activities

Ocho Rios' beautiful seas and diverse marine life make it an excellent choice for water sports and aquatic excursions. Whether you're a thrill-seeker looking for adrenaline-pumping activities or a nature lover eager to discover the undersea world, Ocho Rios has a wide range of water sports and activities to suit every interest and ability level.

Snorkeling: Ocho Rios is home to some of the Caribbean's most stunning coral reefs, making it an ideal location for snorkelers. Grab your mask, snorkel, and fins and plunge under the surface to see a rainbow of colorful fish, beautiful coral formations, and marine life in their natural home. Dunn's River Beach, Mahogany Beach, and Reggae Beach are popular snorkeling destinations, with crystal-clear waters and an abundance of marine life to explore.

Scuba Diving: For skilled divers seeking deeper experiences, Ocho Rios has a variety of diving spots brimming with marine species and undersea delights. Dive operators and dive shops in the vicinity provide guided tours to coral reefs, shipwrecks, and underwater caverns teeming with tropical fish, sea turtles, and other intriguing marine creatures. Whether you're a beginner or an experienced diver, Ocho Rios provides unique diving experiences for all ability levels.

Jet Skiing: Experience the excitement of the open sea by zipping across the waves on a high-speed jet ski experience. Rent a jet ski from one of the beachfront operators and cruise around the glistening seas of Ocho Rios' coastline, taking in panoramic views of the shoreline and lush tropical scenery. Jet skiing is an exciting way to explore the coastline, have adrenaline-fueled fun, and make long-lasting memories with friends and family.

Parasailing: Take to the sky and soar over Ocho Rios' breathtaking coastline on a thrilling parasailing adventure. Strap into a harness, launch from the back of a boat, and soar into the air for bird's-eye views of the turquoise seas below and the lush landscapes that spread to the horizon. Parasailing provides a new viewpoint on Ocho Rios' natural beauty, making it an exciting experience for explorers of all ages.

Kayaking and paddleboarding: For a more relaxing aquatic experience, enjoy Ocho Rios' peaceful waters on a kayak or paddleboard. Rent equipment from seaside sellers and go on a self-guided paddle around the coast, passing by secret coves, mangrove woods, and isolated beaches. Kayaking and paddleboarding allow you to reconnect with nature, take in the tranquil settings, and unwind on the water.

Fishing Excursions: Go on a fishing tour and throw your line into the abundant waters of Ocho Rios, which is known for its rich fishing grounds and numerous marine animals. Join a guided fishing trip and set sail in search of trophy-sized marlin, mahi-mahi, tuna, and other desirable game fish that live in the deep seas off the coast of Ocho Rios. Whether you're an experienced angler or a beginner, Ocho Rios provides unrivaled fishing possibilities for fishermen of all ability levels.

Glass-Bottom Boat Tours: Enjoy the splendor of Ocho Rios' underwater environment without getting wet on a thrilling glass-bottom boat trip. Climb aboard a glass-bottom boat and cruise around the coast, peeking through the clear bottom to see vibrant coral reefs, tropical fish, and other marine life flourishing under the surface. Glass-bottom boat excursions are a fun and instructive way to explore Ocho Rios' marine ecology and learn about the many different animals that live there.

Sunset Cruises: Relax and enjoy the beauty of Ocho Rios' coastline with a magnificent sunset sail along the Caribbean Sea. Set sail on a luxury catamaran or sailboat as the sun sets, coloring the sky in gold, pink, and orange. Relax on deck with a delicious drink in hand, feeling the soothing sea wind on your skin, and taking in the magnificent atmosphere of a Caribbean sunset. Sunset cruises are a romantic and unique way to commemorate important events or simply relax and reconnect with loved ones while admiring the beauty of Ocho Rios' coastline.

Beach Safety Tips.

While Ocho Rios' beaches provide several options for leisure and adventure, emphasizing safety is critical to ensuring a memorable and comfortable beachside experience. Here are crucial beach safety recommendations to remember during your vacation to Ocho Rios:

Swim Near Lifeguard Stations: When feasible, swim at beaches that have lifeguards on duty. Lifeguard stations are deliberately situated in places with safer swimming conditions to give prompt aid in the event of an emergency or crisis.

Respect Beach Flags and Signs: Pay special attention to beach flags and signs that indicate water conditions, risks, or forbidden activities. Red flags indicate dangerous currents or turbulent seas, and warning signs warn beachgoers of potential hazards such as strong currents, jellyfish, or deadly marine life.

Swim with a buddy: Always swim with someone, especially in new water. Swimming with a buddy provides mutual support and aid in case of an emergency, lowering the chance of accidents or injuries. Also, keep an eye out for one another and convey any worries or discomforts while in the water.

Stay Hydrated and Use Sun Protection: To protect yourself from the sun's damaging rays, apply sunscreen liberally, wear UV-protective eyewear, and wear a wide-brimmed hat. Stay hydrated by drinking enough of water, especially in hot and humid weather, to avoid dehydration and heat-related disorders.

Be Aware of Rip Currents: Rip currents are powerful and narrow channels of water that move seaward from the land. If you get caught in a rip current, don't panic. Instead of swimming against the river, swim parallel to the coastline until you're free of its draw. Once you're free of the current, swim diagonally back to shore.

Know Your Limits: Evaluate and recognize your swimming talents accurately. If you are not a confident swimmer, avoid swimming in deep water or strong currents. Stick to specified swimming locations and avoid exploring regions that offer hazards beyond your ability.

Supervise youngsters Closely: Keep an eye on youngsters at all times, especially when they are near or in water. Children who are not proficient swimmers should wear proper flotation devices. Educate kids on beach safety principles including obeying flags and remaining in approved swimming zones.

Be Aware of Marine Life: Learn about the most prevalent marine life risks in the region, such as jellyfish, sea urchins, and coral reefs. Avoid touching or disturbing aquatic creatures, since certain species may respond with painful stings or bites if threatened or provoked.

Stay Alert and Prepared: Be aware of changing weather conditions and ocean tides, since they can affect water safety and beach accessibility. If the weather worsens quickly, be prepared to seek shelter or leave the beach.

Emergency Preparedness: Learn about emergency protocols and how to contact local authorities, lifeguards, and medical institutions. Carry a fully charged mobile phone and make sure you can reach emergency services in the event of an accident, injury, or medical emergency.

By following these beach safety precautions and practicing caution while exploring Ocho Rios' beautiful beaches, you may reduce dangers and guarantee a safe and pleasurable beach experience for yourself and your friends. Prioritize safety, respect the environment, and enjoy the beauty of Ocho Rios' coastal treasures responsibly.

Chapter 5

MUST-SEE ATTRACTIONS IN OCHO RIOS

Ocho Rios, tucked along Jamaica's magnificent north coast, entices visitors with its intriguing combination of natural beauty, cultural legacy, and thrilling activities.

In this chapter, we look at the must-see sites that characterize Ocho Rios' charm and provide remarkable experiences for people of all ages and interests. Ocho Rios is packed with renowned attractions, including flowing waterfalls, verdant jungles, and encounters with marine life.

Dunn's River Falls

Dunn's River Falls is one of Jamaica's most recognizable natural beauties and a must-see site for tourists visiting Ocho Rios. Dunn's River Falls, which cascades over 180 meters (600 feet) in a succession of tiered limestone stairs, is both stunning and exciting. Here's all you need know about this iconic attraction:

Natural Beauty: Dunn's River Falls is well-known for its stunning beauty, with crystal-clear waters falling over natural rock formations amid lush tropical foliage. The falls' tiered form provides gorgeous pools and cascades, beckoning tourists to explore and immerse themselves in nature's beauty.

Climbing the Falls: One of the joys of a trip to Dunn's River Falls is the ability to ascend its breathtaking tiers. Visitors may ascend the waterfall's terraced stairs with skilled guides, navigating between the rushing waters and natural ponds. The ascent is both exhilarating and energizing, with breathtaking views of the surrounding environment and the Caribbean Sea beyond.

Refreshing Swim: After the thrilling climb, tourists may cool off and unwind in the refreshing waters at the base of the falls. The cold, refreshing waters give the ideal reprieve from the tropical heat, enabling tourists to swim, wade, and enjoy the natural beauty of the area.

Surrounding Attractions: In addition to the falls, Dunn's River Falls Park provides a variety of facilities and activities for guests to enjoy. Explore the park's gorgeous gardens, picnic spaces, and gift stores, or eat great Jamaican food at the on-site restaurant.

Visitors' Tips: To get the most of your visit to Dunn's River Falls, consider wearing water shoes or strong footwear with high traction to negotiate the treacherous rocks. It's also a good idea to bring a waterproof camera to record those memorable moments as you approach the falls.

Dunn's River Falls is not just a natural wonder, but also a representation of Jamaica's beauty and strength. A visit to this legendary destination guarantees a memorable trip and the opportunity to engage with the natural marvels of the Caribbean.

Mystic Mountain

For those looking for excitement and adrenaline-pumping thrills, Mystic Mountain is a must-see in Ocho Rios. Mystic Mountain, set against a natural rainforest setting, provides an exciting selection of activities and experiences for both nature lovers and adventure enthusiasts:

Sky Explorer: Begin your adventure to Mystic Mountain's peak on the Sky Explorer, a cutting-edge chairlift that ascends through the rainforest canopy. As you soar easily aloft, take in panoramic views of the lush terrain below and see the spectacular beauty of Ocho Rios' coastline landscapes.

Bobsled Jamaica: Bring out your inner Jamaican bobsledder with an exciting ride on the Bobsled Jamaica attraction. Inspired by the island's renowned bobsled team, this gravity-driven thrill coaster weaves through twists and turns as it descends the mountain slopes, providing an adrenaline-fueled trip for thrill-seekers of all ages.

Canopy Zip Line: For an adrenaline rush like no other, take a thrilling zip line journey through the rainforest canopy. Participants on zip lines glide through the treetops, suspended high above the forest floor, taking in bird's-eye views of the rich greenery and various fauna below.

Mystic Pavilion: Visit the Mystic Pavilion, a thriving center of culture, history, and entertainment at the peak of Mystic Mountain. Discover Jamaica's rich past via interactive exhibitions, cultural displays, and live performances that highlight the island's music, dance, and folklore.

Nature paths: Take a leisurely stroll along Mystic Mountain's network of nature paths, which snake through the rainforest. Keep a watch out for natural flora and animals, such as tropical birds, butterflies, and exotic plant species that flourish in this biodiverse habitat.

Dining and Shopping: After a day of action, relax and refuel at the Mystic Mountain restaurant, where you can enjoy wonderful Jamaican food and cool tropical beverages while admiring the panoramic views of the surrounding countryside. Browse the onsite gift shop for souvenirs, handicrafts, and locally manufactured things to remember your visit to Mystic Mountain.

Mystic Mountain provides a spectacular combination of adventure, nature, and culture, immersing guests in the beauty and diversity of Jamaica's natural environment.

Dolphin Cove.

Dolphin Cove is Ocho Rios' leading marine attraction, providing tourists with an immersive encounter with aquatic life situated in a lovely tropical environment. Here's why Dolphin Cove is a must-see site for travelers:

Swim with Dolphins: Immerse yourself in the exciting world of marine animals by swimming and interacting with dolphins in their natural environment. Dolphin Cove offers a range of participatory events in which guests may frolic, dance, and even receive a dolphin kiss under the supervision of trained trainers.

Stingray interactions: In addition to dolphin interactions, Dolphin Cove offers guests the opportunity to meet and engage with other intriguing aquatic species such as stingrays. Enter the small lagoon to see the gracefulness of these beautiful creatures while learning about their habits and conservation efforts.

Shark Encounters: For the daring at heart, Dolphin Cove gives the opportunity to participate in a spectacular shark encounter. Step into the shark cage and witness these majestic predators up close, getting crucial insights about their behavior and the conservation work underway to safeguard these vital marine species.

Exotic Bird Aviary: Discover the exotic bird aviary tucked within Dolphin Cove's beautiful surroundings. Witness a kaleidoscope of colors as tropical bird species from Jamaica and beyond fly and sing among the lush vegetation. Stroll around the botanical gardens, admiring the different flora and creatures that make this refuge home.

Nature paths and Mini Zoo: Walk along magnificent nature paths that run through the lush surroundings of Dolphin Cove. Meet indigenous species such as iguanas, snakes, and exotic birds, and learn about Jamaica's vast biodiversity and the importance of conservation efforts.

Educational talks: At Dolphin Cove, marine biologists and animal care professionals will provide educational talks and participatory demonstrations. Learn about marine life's behavior, physiology, and conservation status, which will help you appreciate the delicate balance of ocean ecosystems.

Photographic and Souvenirs: Professional photographic services are available on site to help you capture cherished memories of your Dolphin Cove trip. Browse the gift shop for interesting gifts and mementos to mark your visit to this spectacular marine refuge.

Dolphin Cove provides a riveting combination of education, conservation, and remarkable experiences, giving guests a better appreciation of marine life and the need of protecting our oceans.

Chapter 6

CULTURAL EXPERIENCES IN OCHO RIOS.

Ocho Rios is a dynamic hub of Jamaican culture and heritage, as well as a destination for beachgoers and adventurers alike. Immerse yourself in Ocho Rios' cultural attractions, which include lively markets and excellent cuisine, as well as the throbbing rhythms of reggae music and dance.

In this chapter, we will look at the various cultural experiences that Ocho Rios has to offer visitors.

Local Markets and Craft Stores

Exploring the local markets and craft shops in Ocho Rios provides an intriguing look into Jamaican culture and craftsmanship. From bustling street markets to artisanal boutiques, here's where you can find real goods and immerse yourself in local culture:

Ocho Rios Craft Market: Situated in the middle of town, the Ocho Rios Craft Market is a thriving hub of activity where artisans display their handcrafted items. Browse among vendors selling vibrant textiles, wood carvings, pottery, jewelry, and other locally crafted items. Engage in friendly haggling and discussion with vendors, and bring home a piece of Jamaican culture as a treasured souvenir of your trip.

Island Village Craft Market: Located near the cruise ship terminal, Island Village Craft Market sells a wide variety of artisanal goods and handicrafts. Discover a carefully picked assortment of handmade products, such as woven baskets, straw hats, paintings, and traditional Jamaican spices and sauces. As you stroll through the market's bustling pathways, take in the lively atmosphere and listen to live music and cultural activities.

Harmony Hall Art Gallery: Harmony Hall Art Gallery, located near Ocho Rios, offers a more upmarket shopping experience. This exquisite gallery displays the works of local and foreign artists, including paintings, sculptures, and mixed-media pieces inspired by Jamaican culture and Caribbean landscapes. Admire the skill and creativity on show, and maybe even buy a masterpiece to decorate your home.

Exploring Ocho Rios' local markets and craft shops allows you to support local artisans, learn about Jamaican culture, and find one-of-a-kind souvenirs that capture the essence of the island.

Jamaican Cuisine and Dining Experience

No trip to Ocho Rios is complete without sampling the delectable flavors of Jamaican cuisine. Jamaican cuisine is a sensory delight, with fiery jerk chicken, delicious fish, and tropical fruits. Here are a few gastronomic experiences to enjoy in Ocho Rios:

Jerk Centers: Try Jamaica's distinctive cuisine, jerk chicken, at one of the island's well-known jerk centers. Jerk chicken is savory and aromatic, marinated in a blend of spices such as scotch bonnet peppers, allspice, and thyme, and slow-cooked over open flames for a smoky, rich finish. For a really authentic Jamaican supper, serve jerk chicken alongside typical side dishes such as rice and peas, festival (sweet fried dumplings), and fried plantains.

Fish Delights: Ocho Rios' beachfront location provides a variety of fresh fish delicacies. Enjoy grilled lobster, fried fish, and shrimp cooked in a range of delectable sauces, from garlic butter to coconut curry. Savor the colorful flavors of the sea while dining al fresco, overlooking the dazzling Caribbean waves, with a refreshing tropical drink or freshly squeezed fruit juice.

Local Eateries & Street Food: Wander the streets of Ocho Rios to find hidden gems serving delicious Jamaican cuisine. From roadside jerk shops to family-owned eateries, Ocho Rios has a rich gastronomic landscape ready to be discovered. Sample classic foods like ackee and saltfish (Jamaica's national dish), curry goat, and escovitch fish to experience the real flavors of Jamaica's rich culinary heritage.

Cooking workshops and Culinary Tours: Learn more about Jamaican food with hands-on cooking workshops and culinary tours in Ocho Rios. Learn the secrets of traditional Jamaican cuisine from local chefs, including how to make jerk marinades, coconut-infused curries, and delectable desserts like rum cake and coconut drops. Guided culinary trips to lively markets and local farms allow you to acquire fresh ingredients while learning about Jamaica's diverse food culture.

Jamaican cuisine reflects the island's rich cultural background and diverse culinary influences, with dishes ranging from savory jerk chicken to exquisite seafood and exotic fruits. Enjoy the flavors of Jamaica and travel on a culinary journey that will excite your taste senses and leave you wanting more.

Reggae Music and Dance Culture.

Reggae music and dance culture are strongly engrained in Jamaican society, with Ocho Rios serving as a thriving hub for the island's musical legacy. From vibrant dance halls to pulsating reggae clubs, here's where you can feel Jamaica's rhythmic heartbeat:

Live Music Venues: Immerse yourself in the soul-stirring sounds of reggae music in live music venues and clubs all across Ocho Rios. From small seaside pubs to lively nightclubs, Ocho Rios has a wide range of locations where you may dance to the beats of live bands and local musicians. Dance the night away to legendary reggae, ska, and dancehall hits, and feel the addictive energy of Jamaica's music industry.

Reggae Festivals & Events: Schedule your vacation around one of Ocho Rios' exciting reggae festivals and events, where you can celebrate the island's musical heritage against a backdrop of sun, beach, and sea. From the annual Reggae Sumfest to the Rebel Salute music festival, Ocho Rios features a range of events featuring Jamaica's best reggae singers and entertainers. Join fellow music aficionados from all around the world as you groove to the rhythms of reggae, dancehall, and roots music while immersing yourself in Jamaica's rich culture.

Bob Marley Museum and Tribute: Visit Ocho Rios' Bob Marley Museum and Tribute to honor the renowned King of Reggae. Explore Bob Marley's life and legacy via interactive exhibitions, memorabilia, and multimedia displays that chart his incredible rise from humble beginnings to international stardom. Learn about the significance of reggae music as a tool for social change and cultural expression, as well as Bob Marley's lasting impact on music, politics, and popular culture around the world.

Dancehall Parties and Sound Systems: Local parties and sound system events in Ocho Rios offer an exhilarating glimpse into Jamaica's dancehall scene. Dancehall music, with its throbbing beats and captivating rhythms, is a dynamic reflection of Jamaican youth culture and urban life. Join the party on the dance floor as you move to the latest dancehall music and vintage hits, and experience the dynamic art of dancehall dancing firsthand. From daggering to bruk out, dancehall exemplifies Jamaican street culture's originality, passion, and raw energy.

Reggae Dance courses: Immerse yourself in the world of reggae music and dance with interactive dance courses available in Ocho Rios. Learn the trademark motions and rhythms of reggae dancehall, ska, and roots reggae with the help of expert instructors. Whether you're a novice or an experienced dancer, reggae dance courses are a fun and engaging way to engage with Jamaican culture and express yourself through movement and song.

Reggae music and dance culture are essential components of Jamaica's identity and soul, expressing the tenacity, ingenuity, and vibrancy of its people. Embrace the reggae sounds, experience the dancehall pulse, and immerse yourself in Ocho Rios' unique cultural tapestry.

Chapter 7

OUTDOOR ADVENTURES IN OCHO RIOS

Ocho Rios, with its lush landscapes and unspoiled natural beauty, is an ideal destination for outdoor enthusiasts looking for adrenaline-pumping adventures and immersive nature experiences. Ocho Rios has everything for any adventurer, from hiking rainforest trails to ziplining through the canopy and going on exhilarating ATV excursions.

In this chapter, we look at the thrilling outdoor adventures that await in this tropical paradise.

Rainforest Hiking Trails

Immerse yourself in the spectacular beauty of Ocho Rios' rainforests on a memorable hiking excursion. From casual strolls to strenuous treks, here are some of the most interesting rainforest hiking routes to discover:

Blue Mountains Trail: Take a hike through the UNESCO-listed Blue and John Crow Mountains National Park, which is home to some of Jamaica's most pristine rainforests. Ascend through lush flora, towering bamboo groves, and flowing waterfalls to the peak of Blue Mountain Peak, the island's highest point. Admire magnificent views of the surrounding mountains and the Caribbean Sea, and learn about the diverse species that lives in this ecological treasure.

Mystic Mountain Trails: Discover the delights of Mystic Mountain's rainforest trails, where adventure and nature coexist harmoniously. Choose from a number of guided hiking trails that lead through lush vegetation, ancient trees, and hidden waterfalls. Keep an eye out for native wildlife such as tropical birds, butterflies, and endemic plant species as you walk through this nature sanctuary's challenging terrain.

Coyaba River Garden Trail: Discover the magnificent sceneries of Coyaba River Garden and Museum, a peaceful oasis set among Ocho Rios' green hills. Wander down winding roads shaded by towering trees, where you'll find beautiful botanical gardens, tranquil water features, and colorful tropical blossoms around every corner. Follow the leisurely flow of the Coyaba River through the garden, which provides moments of quiet and introspection amidst Jamaica's natural splendor.

Konoko Falls Nature Trail: Take a guided stroll through the picturesque sceneries of Konoko Falls and Park, where thick rainforest plants and flowing waterfalls await discovery. Trek to the spectacular Konoko Falls over well-maintained trails that snake through dense vegetation, limestone outcrops, and natural pools. Take a relaxing dip in the cool, crystal-clear waters of the falls, or simply relax and reconnect with nature.

Rainforest hiking paths in Ocho Rios provide a riveting blend of adventure, exploration, and natural beauty, allowing outdoor enthusiasts to immerse themselves in Jamaica's unspoiled environment.

Zipline and Canopy Tours

Exhilarating ziplining and canopy tours allow you to soar through the treetops and explore the lush canopy of Ocho Rios. Here's what you should know about these thrilling adventures:

Chukka Caribbean Adventures: Take a ziplining trip with Chukka Caribbean Adventures, one of Ocho Rios' top adventure tour operators. Glide through the canopy on a series of ziplines, passing through lush valleys, flowing rivers, and tropical landscapes with stunning views of the surroundings. Feel the rush of excitement as you zip from platform to platform, enjoying the thrill of flying in the natural beauty of Jamaica's rainforests.

Mystic Mountain Zipline: Embark on a thrilling ride through the jungle canopy of Ocho Rios. Strap into a harness and soar through the air on a network of ziplines that connect suspension bridges and platforms high above the forest floor. Feel the wind in your hair and the adrenaline rush through your veins as you take in the panoramic views of Mystic Mountain and the Caribbean Sea beyond.

Canopy excursions: Experience the beauty of Ocho Rios' rainforest canopy on guided canopy excursions that provide a unique perspective on Jamaica's natural surroundings. Explore elevated walkways and swinging bridges perched among the treetops, marveling at the rich flora and creatures that survive in this biodiverse environment. As you explore Jamaica's rainforests from above, you'll learn about the importance of canopy conservation and environmental care.

Ziplining and canopy tours in Ocho Rios are an exciting way to see the beauty and richness of Jamaica's rainforests, leaving travelers with lasting memories and spectacular views of the island's natural surroundings.

Safari Excursions with ATVs and Jeeps

Off-road adventurers may explore Ocho Rios' mountainous terrain on thrilling ATV and Jeep safari adventures. Here's what you can anticipate from these adrenaline-fueled activities:

ATV Adventures: Unleash your inner adventurer with ATV tours that take you off the beaten path and into the heart of Ocho Rios wilderness. Climb aboard a tough ATV and negotiate steep slopes, muddy paths, and dense vegetation to discover hidden nooks of the island that traditional vehicles cannot reach. Experience the thrill of off-road exploration as you travel through different landscapes, from lush jungles to harsh slopes, uncovering hidden gems along the way.

Jeep Safari Tours: Take a Jeep safari tour and explore Ocho Rios' stunning landscapes and cultural landmarks. Get into a strong 4x4 vehicle and head off the usual path, taking scenic routes through rural communities, green valleys, and breathtaking views. Learn about Jamaica's rich history, culture, and traditions from professional guides while immersing yourself in the real sights and sounds of island life.

River Crossings and Waterfalls: On ATV and Jeep safari excursions, you will bridge rivers and ford streams while exploring the harsh landscape of Ocho Rios' interior. Cool down with pleasant dips in natural pools and waterfalls, where you may swim, splash, and soak in the revitalizing waters of Jamaica's pristine rivers. Admire the beauty of flowing waterfalls like Dunn's River Falls and Blue Hole, and create unforgettable memories amidst the island's stunning surroundings.

ATV and Jeep safari tours are an exciting way to explore Ocho Rios' natural marvels and hidden treasures, giving travelers with an unforgettable off-road experience.

Chapter 8

EXPLORING OCHO RIOS' WATERFALLS.

Ocho Rios, known for its natural beauty and lush surroundings, is home to some of Jamaica's most stunning waterfalls. Ocho Rios' waterfalls range from hidden gems concealed in the rainforest to iconic cascades framed by towering cliffs, providing visitors with a refreshing escape into the island's unspoiled wildlife.

In this chapter, we'll explore the amazing beauty and charm of Ocho Rios' most captivating waterfalls.

Blue Hole.

Blue Hole, nestled in the luscious hills of Ocho Rios, is a hidden gem that entices visitors with its crystalline waters, lush surroundings, and tranquil atmosphere. Here's all you should know about exploring Blue Hole:

Natural Oasis: Blue Hole, nestled in the center of the rainforest, is a natural oasis distinguished by its azure waters, limestone formations, and lush vegetation. The quiet setting provides a peaceful respite from the hustle and bustle of Ocho Rios, allowing tourists to unwind and reconnect with nature.

Swimming and Cliff Jumping: Blue Hole is famous for its pleasant swimming holes and thrilling cliff jumping sites. Dive into the Blue Hole's delightful waters and swim in its cool, crystal-clear pools, which are surrounded by lush flora and waterfalls. For the more brave adventurers, try your courage by diving from the surrounding cliffs into the deep, blue waters below, feeling an amazing surge of adrenaline while immersed in the natural beauty of the rainforest.

Guided Tours and Nature Walks: Experience the beauty of Blue Hole through guided tours and nature walks led by knowledgeable local guides. Discover hidden routes that lead through the rainforest, offering breathtaking views, unusual plants, and native species along the way. Discover the biological significance of Blue Hole and the importance of conservation efforts to protect this pristine natural gem for future generations to enjoy.

Picnic spaces and Facilities: Blue Hole has picnic spaces and facilities where guests may unwind and spend the day in the splendor of the rainforest. Pack a picnic lunch and relax in the shade of towering trees while listening to the relaxing sounds of tumbling waterfalls and chirping birds. On-site facilities include changing rooms, bathrooms, and refreshment outlets for enhanced convenience and comfort.

Exploring Blue Hole provides a revitalizing getaway into nature, allowing guests to immerse themselves in the peace and beauty of Ocho Rios' unspoiled jungle setting.

Konoko Falls.

Konoko Falls, located on the outskirts of Ocho Rios, is a stunning waterfall surrounded by lush botanical gardens, towering trees, and exotic flora. Here's what to expect when you visit Konoko Falls:

Scenic Beauty: Konoko Falls is well-known for its scenic beauty and serene atmosphere, making it a favorite destination for nature lovers and adventurers alike. Surrounded by lush flora and tropical blossoms, the falling waters of Konoko Falls form a stunning spectacle against the backdrop of the rainforest, providing tourists with a peaceful retreat into nature's embrace.

Guided Tours and Nature Walks: Experience the wonders of Konoko Falls through guided tours and nature walks lead by knowledgeable guides. Wander along well-kept trails that lead through the botanical gardens, presenting a broad range of plant species such as orchids, heliconia, and bamboo groves.

Learn about Konoko Falls' cultural significance and role in Jamaican history and mythology, getting insight into the island's rich legacy and natural beauties.

Waterfall Climbs and Swimming lakes: Climb the tiers of Konoko Falls on guided waterfall hikes that lead to natural lakes and swimming holes hidden in the rainforest. Take a pleasant plunge in the cool, clear waters of the falls, which are surrounded by lush flora and peaceful natural noises. Whether you're swimming in the pools or admiring the cascades, Konoko Falls provides a refreshing respite from the heat and humidity of the tropics.

Cultural and Historical Attractions: In addition to its natural beauty, Konoko Falls has cultural and historical attractions that shed light on Jamaica's history and present. Explore the Taino Museum, which houses relics and displays on the island's indigenous history. Wander through the aviary and reptile park, home to native birds, reptiles, and tropical fauna, and learn about the unique ecosystems that thrive in Konoko Falls' lush environs.

Konoko Falls is a mesmerizing site that enchants tourists with its natural splendor, cultural history, and tranquil ambiance, providing a wonderful experience for nature lovers and explorers of all ages.

Reach Falls.

Reach Falls, located in the green jungles of Jamaica's eastern coast, is a hidden gem waiting to be discovered by adventurers seeking solitude and natural beauty. Here's a closer look at why Reach Falls is a must-see destination:

Natural Beauty: Reach Falls is a beautiful cascade of water that flows over limestone cliffs, creating a succession of dazzling pools tucked among lush flora. The falls are surrounded by tall trees, ferns, and bright tropical foliage, providing a tranquil sanctuary in the midst of the rainforest. Visitors are met by the calming sounds of falling water and the fresh aroma of the forest, allowing them to relax and appreciate nature.

Guided Tours and Eco-Adventures: Learn about the delights of Reach Falls through guided tours and eco-adventures offered by expert locals. Explore gorgeous routes through the jungle, discovering secret waterfalls, natural caverns, and crystal-clear pools along the way. Learn about the area's vast biodiversity, from endemic plant species to exotic wildlife, and develop an understanding of Jamaica's delicate natural balance.

Waterfall Climbs and Swimming Holes: Guided waterfall climbs allow adventurers to explore isolated pools and cascades hidden among the thick greenery. Take a refreshing plunge in the falls' cool, green waters, surrounded by the natural splendor of the rainforest. Swim beneath the flowing waves and feel the soft caress of the water against your skin, providing a refreshing respite from the heat and humidity of the tropical climate.

Cave investigation and Photography: Take a cave investigation excursion to discover hidden chambers and underground corridors cut into the limestone cliffs of Reach Falls. Marvel at the ancient rock formations and geological wonders beneath the surface, which are illuminated by the mellow glow of natural light filtering through the canopy above. Capture amazing images of the falls and surrounding surroundings to remember your tour through Jamaica's wildness.

Picnic spots and Facilities: Reach Falls provides picnic spots and facilities for tourists to relax and unwind while admiring the beauty of the rainforest. Pack a picnic lunch and enjoy a leisurely meal surrounded by nature's sights and sounds, or simply relax and soak up the peace. On-site amenities include changing rooms, restrooms, and refreshment outlets, making it easier for guests to see Reach Falls.

Reach Falls is a secret sanctuary waiting to be discovered, providing a peaceful escape into Jamaica's natural beauties. Whether you're swimming in the chilly waters, exploring hidden caverns, or simply relaxing in the woods, Reach Falls provides a memorable experience amidst the grandeur of the Caribbean countryside.

Chapter 9

FAMILY-FRIENDLY ACTIVITIES IN OCHO RIOS

Ocho Rios is not just a haven for adventurers and beachgoers, but also an excellent choice for families vacationing with children. Ocho Rios has a wide range of activities for guests of all ages, including touring botanical gardens, horseback riding trips, and resting on family-friendly beaches.

In this chapter, we will look at the family-friendly attractions and experiences available in Ocho Rios.

Turtle River Park

Turtle River Park is a huge sanctuary tucked in the center of Ocho Rios, providing families with a beautiful blend of natural beauty, recreational activities, and educational opportunities. Here's what to expect when you visit Turtle River Park with your family:

Botanical Gardens: Explore Turtle River Park's magnificent botanical gardens, which feature a broad collection of tropical plants, flowers, and trees. Wander along meandering paths lined with towering palms, vivid blossoms, and exotic flora, discovering hidden jewels at every turn. As you visit the gardens, you will be able to admire the beauty of orchids, bromeliads, and ferns while also learning about Jamaica's diverse botanical heritage.

Turtle River: Follow the calm flow of the Turtle River through the park, which provides a peaceful backdrop for leisurely strolls and picnics. Cross quaint wooden bridges to enjoy the peaceful waters teeming with fish, turtles, and other aquatic life. Take a guided boat tour along the river to experience the natural splendor of Ocho Rios' lush sceneries while learning about the ecosystem and creatures that call Turtle River Park home.

Children's Playground: Let the kids burn off energy on the children's playground, which has swings, slides, and climbing structures built for safe and fun play. Watch as kids discover the playground's interactive features and meet new friends amidst the joy and excitement of outdoor play. The playground provides a pleasant and engaging environment for children to unwind and enjoy the great outdoors while their parents relax nearby.

Educational Programs and Events: Turtle River Park offers a variety of educational programs and events that engage and inspire visitors of all ages. Join trained park rangers on guided nature walks to learn about the flora and wildlife of Jamaica, as well as conservation initiatives to safeguard the country's natural legacy. Participate in hands-on seminars, interactive exhibitions, and eco-friendly activities that encourage environmental stewardship and sustainability.

Turtle River Park provides a harmonic blend of environment, recreation, and education, making it an ideal destination for families looking to reconnect with nature and share memorable experiences.

Horseback Riding Tours.

Take your family on an exciting horseback riding experience through the picturesque splendor of Ocho Rios' countryside and beaches. What to expect from horseback riding trips in Ocho Rios:

Scenic routes: Follow scenic routes through Ocho Rios' beautiful environments, which range from lush jungles to pristine beaches and coastal cliffs. Enjoy breathtaking views of the Caribbean Sea and the surrounding countryside as you wander along peaceful paths, surrounded by nature's sights and sounds.

Guided Tours: Participate in guided horseback riding tours conducted by expert equestrian guides who will provide a safe and pleasurable experience for riders of all abilities. Discover Jamaica's rich equestrian legacy and the history of horseback riding on the island while exploring hidden trails and off-the-beaten-path spots.

Beach Rides: Feel the thrill of riding down the sandy sands of Ocho Rios' most beautiful beaches, where the warm Caribbean breeze caresses your skin and the rhythmic rhythm of the waves beneath your feet. Trot along the water's edge and enjoy spectacular views of the coastline, pausing to splash in the surf or observe the surroundings.

Family-Friendly Options: Horseback riding trips in Ocho Rios are ideal for riders of all ages, including children and beginners. Choose from a selection of tour packages and ride durations, ranging from short excursions to full-day experiences, to ensure that everyone has something to love.

Horseback riding trips offer a unique opportunity for families to bond, enjoy the natural beauty of Ocho Rios, and make lasting memories together in the breathtaking magnificence of Jamaica's countryside and beaches.

Family-Friendly Beaches.

Ocho Rios has some of Jamaica's most beautiful and family-friendly beaches, with soft sand, calm waves, and a variety of recreational activities for guests of all ages. Here are some of the best family-friendly beaches to visit in Ocho Rios:

Turtle Beach: located on Jamaica's gorgeous north coast, is a picturesque stretch of golden sand surrounded by crystal-clear waters and swaying palm trees. The beach has quiet, shallow waters excellent for swimming and wading, making it a favorite destination for families with young children. Rent a beach umbrella and lounge chair and relax in the sun, or go snorkeling to see the adjacent coral reefs.

Dunn's River Beach: Adjacent to the famous Dunn's River Falls, Dunn's River Beach is a thriving hub of activity and excitement, with a variety of family-friendly amenities and attractions. Swim in the soothing waters of the Caribbean Sea, take a guided climb up the famed falls, or simply relax on the sun-kissed beaches and watch cruise ships sail into dock. Dunn's River Beach, with its vibrant environment and breathtaking natural beauty, is a must-see site for families visiting Ocho Rios.

Mahogany Beach: Mahogany Beach, located in a hidden cove just minutes from downtown Ocho Rios, provides a peaceful respite from the city's rush and bustle. The beach has quiet, clear seas that are ideal for swimming and snorkeling, as well as a variety of water sports and recreational activities for people of all ages. Rent a kayak or paddleboard to explore the coastline, or simply rest on the soft beaches and soak up the laid-back atmosphere of this hidden gem.

James Bond Beach: Named after the renowned fictional spy, James Bond Beach is a pristine stretch of shoreline with calm waves and breathtaking vistas of the Caribbean Sea. The beach has a variety of family-friendly attractions, such as picnic spaces, playgrounds, and beach volleyball courts, so there's something for everyone. Swim in the quiet, turquoise seas, create sandcastles with the youngsters, or simply relax and enjoy the gorgeous beauty that surrounds you.

Family-friendly beaches in Ocho Rios provide the ideal setting for a day of sun, sand, and sea, with a plethora of recreational activities and services to keep the entire family entertained and involved. Whether you're swimming, snorkeling, or simply soaking up the sun, Ocho Rios' beaches offer limitless hours of entertainment and leisure for people of all ages.

Chapter 10

NIGHTLIFE & ENTERTAINMENT IN OCHO RIOS.

As the sun sets over the Caribbean Sea, Ocho Rios comes alive with a thriving nightlife culture that invites tourists to dance, dine, and soak up the island's infectious energy. From throbbing nightclubs to intimate live music venues and intriguing cultural acts, Ocho Rios has something for everyone's taste and mood.

In this chapter, we'll look into Ocho Rios' broad and vibrant nightlife, where the fun never stops and the memories last a lifetime.

Bars and Nightclubs

Ocho Rios has a vibrant and eclectic mix of pubs and nightclubs where residents and visitors alike gather to celebrate life and dance the night away. Here's a look at the explosive nightlife scene in Ocho Rios:

Amnesia Nightclub: Located in the center of Ocho Rios, Amnesia Nightclub is a premier nightlife destination noted for its lively ambiance, throbbing sounds, and impressive DJ roster. Dance the night away to the newest reggae, dancehall, and soca hits while mixing with a varied throng of partygoers from across the world. With its cutting-edge sound system, brilliant light shows, and active dance floor, Amnesia promises a memorable night of fun and excitement.

Margueritaville Ocho Rios: A popular destination for both visitors and residents, Margueritaville Ocho Rios boasts a laid-back island attitude and a bustling party scene. By day, enjoy tropical beverages, wonderful Jamaican cuisine, and sunbathing on the beachside patio. As night falls, the party heats up with live music, DJ sets, and themed events that keep the dance floor full until early in the morning.

Taj Mahal Shopping Center: The Taj Mahal Shopping Center has a thriving nightlife culture, with a variety of pubs, lounges, and entertainment venues to try. The Taj Mahal provides something for everyone, including rooftop bars with magnificent views of the Caribbean Sea and quiet cocktail lounges with a sophisticated environment. As you explore the diverse flavors of Ocho Rios' nightlife, you can sample exotic beverages, listen to live music, and socialize with locals and other travelers.

Ocean's 11: Located on the Ocho Rios shoreline, Ocean's 11 is a popular hangout for musicians and partygoers. Dance under the stars to the sounds of live bands and DJ sets, or unwind with a refreshing drink and soak up the laid-back island atmosphere. With its prominent location, lively atmosphere, and eclectic musical lineup, Ocean's 11 guarantees an outstanding night of entertainment and excitement.

Whether you want to dance until dawn, drink exotic cocktails, or simply enjoy the colorful atmosphere of Ocho Rios' nightlife, the city's pubs and nightclubs have something for everyone.

Live Music Venues.

Immerse yourself in the soul-stirring sounds of Jamaica's lively music scene at Ocho Rios' live music venues, where brilliant musicians and artists demonstrate their abilities and electrify audiences. Here are some of the best live music venues in Ocho Rios.

Tracks & Records Ocho Rios: Tracks & Records, owned by Jamaican sprinter Usain Bolt, is a bustling sports bar and restaurant that also serves as Ocho Rios' primary live music venue. Dance to the rhythms of reggae, dancehall, and soca music as local bands and performers entertain guests with addictive sounds and deep vocals. Enjoy delicious Jamaican cuisine, distinctive cocktails, and the vibrant atmosphere of this legendary restaurant.

Mongoose Jamaica Jazz & Blues Club: Situated within the Moon Palace Jamaica resort, the Mongoose Jamaica Jazz and Blues Club provides an attractive environment for live music and entertainment. Sit back and relax in the club's quiet lounge area while amazing musicians serenade you with smooth jazz, sensual blues, and deep R&B. Indulge in delicious meals and premium beverages while enjoying an evening of world-class music and hospitality.

Hard Rock Café Ocho Rios: In addition to being a well-known eating destination, Hard Rock Café Ocho Rios is also a thriving live music venue that organizes a range of acts and events all year. From acoustic shows by local artists to high-energy rock concerts with worldwide headliners, Hard Rock Café provides a diverse range of live music experiences for customers to enjoy. Dance, sing along, and create unforgettable moments at this legendary music venue in the center of Ocho Rios.

Oceans on the Ridge: Perched atop a gorgeous ridge overlooking the Ocho Rios beach, Oceans on the Ridge is a picturesque restaurant and live music venue with breathtaking views and amazing performances. Enjoy alfresco eating on the large patio while live bands and solo singers perform reggae, calypso, and jazz music against the backdrop of the Caribbean Sea. Oceans on the Ridge's relaxing atmosphere and stunning views make it ideal for an evening of music, laughing, and celebration.

Live music venues in Ocho Rios offer a diverse range of musical genres and styles, allowing visitors to immerse themselves in the vivid rhythms and melodies of Jamaica's cultural history.

Cultural Performances.

Explore the rich fabric of Jamaican culture through intriguing cultural performances that highlight the island's history, traditions, and artistic manifestations. Ocho Rios provides guests with a taste of Jamaica's diverse legacy through a variety of cultural events, including passionate dance routines and heartfelt musical performances.

Jamaican Folk Singers: The Jamaican Folk Singers deliver fascinating performances that transport you to the heart of Jamaican folklore. Watch expert dancers and musicians hit the stage, honoring the island's cultural essence with rhythmic drumming, lyrical folk tunes, and exciting dance sequences. Experience the contagious energy and passion of Jamaica's music and dance traditions as artists tell stories that have defined the country's character over decades.

Steel Pan Bands: Indulge in the captivating melodies of steel pan music, a traditional Caribbean art form that speaks to the soul. Local steel pan bands in Ocho Rios put on riveting performances that highlight the versatility and originality of steel drums through complicated compositions and energetic rhythms. Steel pan bands provide a harmonic blend of sound that embodies the essence of Jamaican island culture, ranging from traditional calypso to contemporary renditions.

Reggae Revue Shows: Experience the beat and groove of Jamaica's legendary reggae music through electrifying reggae revue shows. Experience live performances that pay tribute to reggae luminaries such as Bob Marley and Jimmy Cliff, as skilled musicians and vocalists light up the stage with soulful renditions and catchy sounds. Feel the spirit of One Love as reggae revue presentations take you on a musical trip through Jamaica's cultural landscape, highlighting the genre's long history and global significance.

Cultural Festivals & Events: Celebrate Jamaica's spirit via cultural festivals and events that highlight the island's vibrant traditions and artistic expressions. From the throbbing rhythms of the Reggae Sumfest to the delectable flavors of the Ocho Rios Jerk Festival, these dynamic festivals bring together locals and visitors in a vibrant tapestry of music, dance, food, and art. Immerse yourself in the sights, sounds, and flavors of Jamaican culture, as each festival transforms into a spectacular celebration of the country's ingenuity and tradition.

Traditional Dance Performances: Treat your senses to traditional dance performances that embody the essence of Jamaican heritage and storytelling. Admire the elegant motions and exquisite footwork of dancers as they express age-old stories and rituals through their craft. Traditional dance performances, from the throbbing beats of the Kumina to the exuberant motions of the Jonkunnu, provide a glimpse into Jamaica's unique cultural mosaic while also highlighting its people's tenacity and ingenuity.

Artisanal Craft Markets: Discover vibrant artisanal craft markets in Ocho Rios, where local artisans demonstrate their skills and traditions via handmade crafts, artworks, and souvenirs. Discover elaborately woven straw baskets, vibrant batik fabrics, and intricately carved wooden sculptures that showcase Jamaica's rich cultural and creative past. Engage with artists as they tell the tales behind their products, providing insight into the traditions and practices passed down through generations.

Cultural performances in Ocho Rios encourage tourists to immerse themselves in Jamaica's soulful rhythms, brilliant colors, and ageless customs, instilling a greater respect for the island's cultural legacy and artistic creativity.

Chapter 11

SHOPPING IN OCHO RIOS.

Ocho Rios is more than simply a sanctuary for adventure and leisure; it's also a shopping haven. From lively artisan markets bursting with colorful wares to sophisticated shopping plazas featuring a mix of local and international brands, Ocho Rios offers a diversified shopping experience to suit every taste and budget.

In this chapter, we'll look at the dynamic shopping scene in Ocho Rios, highlighting the best places to get one-of-a-kind souvenirs, fashionable clothing, and traditional Jamaican crafts.

Ocho Rios Craft Market.

The Ocho Rios Craft Market is a busy marketplace where local craftsmen display their talents and workmanship, selling a diverse range of handmade goods, traditional crafts, and one-of-a-kind souvenirs. Here's what to expect when visiting the Ocho Rios Craft Market:

Handcrafted Treasures: Explore a treasure trove of handcrafted items, such as wooden sculptures, bright paintings, elaborately woven baskets, and handmade jewelry. Local artists practice their craft with expertise and passion, imbuing each work with the spirit and inventiveness of Jamaica's cultural history. The Ocho Rios Craft Market is a treasure trove of unique discoveries, ranging from colorful ceramics to true Rastafarian goods.

Authentic Jamaican delicacies: Visit the craft market's food stalls and merchants to sample Jamaican delicacies. Enjoy freshly prepared Jamaican dishes such as jerk chicken, patties, and fried plantains, relishing the robust spices and rich tastes that define the island's culinary culture. Wash it all down with a cool coconut water or a tropical fruit smoothie, then immerse yourself in the lively sights, sounds, and flavors of Jamaican street food culture.

Negotiation and Bartering: Bargaining is a long-standing tradition at the Ocho Rios Craft Market, where experienced consumers can put their negotiation skills to the test. Engage merchants in casual conversation as you bargain over pricing and look for the greatest discounts on handmade goods and souvenirs. Remember to approach negotiations with a smile and a sense of humor, and you can end up with a great deal and a memorable shopping experience.

Cultural Immersion: Aside from its colorful marketplace atmosphere, the Ocho Rios Craft Market provides a unique opportunity to connect with Jamaica's rich cultural heritage and traditions. Engage with local artists as they tell the tales behind their creations, providing insight into the techniques, symbolism, and meanings incorporated into each piece. Discover Jamaica's history, folklore, and creative tradition as you browse the market's broad selection of crafts and masterpieces.

The Ocho Rios Craft Market is more than simply a shopping destination; it is also a cultural center where tourists can immerse themselves in Jamaican culture and discover the island's artistic character.

Shopping Malls and Plazas.

For those looking for a more modern shopping experience, Ocho Rios has various shopping malls and plazas with a mix of local boutiques, international brands, and high-end retailers. Here are some of the best shopping venues in Ocho Rios:

Island Village: Located on Ocho Rios' scenic shoreline, Island Village is a prominent shopping and entertainment center with a wide variety of shops, restaurants, and attractions. Browse designer shops and specialty businesses that sell anything from clothing and jewelry to souvenirs and gifts.

Relax in the magnificent tropical gardens, watch live performances at the amphitheater, or swim in the sparkling pool overlooking the Caribbean Sea. Island Village offers a quality retail experience with a relaxed island atmosphere.

Taj Mahal Shopping Center: Located in the center of Ocho Rios, the Taj Mahal Shopping Center is a thriving hub of activity and commerce, with a variety of retail establishments, restaurants, and entertainment options. Explore a variety of shops selling clothing, accessories, electronics, and other items, or eat at one of the center's unique restaurants serving foreign and Jamaican cuisine. With its central position and numerous goods, the Taj Mahal Shopping Center offers a convenient and delightful shopping experience for both visitors and locals.

Sonis Plaza: Sonis Plaza is a thriving shopping center located in the heart of downtown Ocho Rios, with a diverse range of stores and services to fulfill every demand. Browse fashion boutiques, souvenir shops, and specialty stores that sell locally manufactured goods and handcrafted crafts. Grab a bite to eat at one of the plaza's casual eateries or cafes, or simply enjoy the vibrant ambiance as you wander the bustling streets and lanes of downtown Ocho Rios.

Ocho Rios Bay Beach Plaza: The Ocho Rios Bay Beach Plaza, which overlooks the gorgeous Ocho Rios Bay Beach, is a delightful retail and dining destination that embodies island living. Boutique businesses sell beachwear, swimwear, and accessories, as well as one-of-a-kind gifts and mementos to remember your trip to Jamaica. After shopping, relax with a leisurely supper at one of the plaza's coastal restaurants, where you can eat fresh seafood and tropical beverages while admiring the magnificent views of the Caribbean Sea.

Local Souvenirs & Gifts

Exploring Ocho Rios is more than simply discovering its natural beauty and cultural delights; it's also about choosing the right souvenir to remember your trip. Ocho Rios has a plethora of local souvenirs and items that embody Jamaican culture and craftsmanship. Here are some popular options to consider.

Jamaican Rum: Indulge in a bottle of true Jamaican rum and take a journey through the country's rich rum legacy. Ocho Rios features a number of rum distilleries and specialist shops where you may try and buy a variety of rum blends. Whether you prefer the smooth elegance of aged rum or the fiery kick of traditional Jamaican rum punch, a bottle of Jamaican rum makes an excellent keepsake or gift to share with loved ones back home.

Blue Mountain Coffee: Get a taste of Jamaica's finest brew with a bag of Blue Mountain Coffee, which is known for its rich flavor and smooth finish. Grown amid the misty slopes of the

Blue Mountains, this quality coffee is appreciated by coffee connoisseurs all around the world. Visit Ocho Rios' local coffee shops and plantations to get freshly roasted beans or ground coffee, and enjoy the distinct scent and flavor profile of Jamaica's most popular export.

Handmade Crafts and Artwork: Discover Jamaica's lively arts and crafts sector by visiting the local markets and galleries dispersed across Ocho Rios. There are plenty of unique and authentic items to uncover, like finely carved wooden sculptures, hand-painted ceramics, and vivid textiles. Support local artisans and craftsmen by purchasing one-of-a-kind works that reflect Jamaica's cultural heritage and creative spirit, and bring home a piece of island artistry that will serve as a treasured remembrance of your visit to Ocho Rios.

Authentic Jamaican Souvenirs: Immerse yourself in Jamaica's cultural tapestry by selecting authentic souvenirs and keepsakes that encapsulate the soul of the island. Browse around stalls and businesses selling a wide range of things, including Bob Marley memorabilia, Rastafarian apparel and accessories, and authentic Jamaican crafts. Whether you want a handcrafted souvenir or a one-of-a-kind piece of Jamaican memorabilia, Ocho Rios has something for everyone, regardless of taste or budget.

Spices and Sauces: Bring the flavors of Jamaica home with a variety of authentic Jamaican spices and sauces. In Ocho Rios, local shops and specialty businesses sell a variety of spices such as jerk seasoning, curry powder, and allspice, as well as spicy sauces and pepper jellies flavored with the island's scorching scotch bonnet peppers. Experiment with Jamaican delicacies in your own kitchen or serve them to friends and family as a tasty memento of your Jamaican trips.

Local Artisanal Products: Buying locally manufactured artisanal products and handicrafts helps to support sustainable and community-driven initiatives. Look for handmade soaps, candles, and skincare products made using natural ingredients obtained from Jamaica's lush surroundings. Choosing artisanal products not only provides you with a one-of-a-kind and ecologically friendly keepsake, but it also helps to support the livelihoods of local artisans and entrepreneurs.

Chapter 12

DAY TRIPS & EXCURSIONS FROM OCHO RIOS

While Ocho Rios has many attractions and activities, stepping beyond its bounds reveals a world of exploration and discovery. From vibrant towns to natural treasures, day tours and excursions from Ocho Rios allow you to immerse yourself in Jamaica's various landscapes, culture, and history.

In this chapter, we'll look at the best day trips and excursions from Ocho Rios, each providing a distinct and engaging experience.

Kingston Day Trip.

Explore Jamaica's lively capital city, Kingston, where history, culture, and urban life collide. From iconic monuments to cultural organizations, a day trip to Kingston provides an insight into the heart and spirit of Jamaica.

Bob Marley Museum: Begin your trip of Kingston by visiting the iconic Bob Marley Museum, which is located in the reggae icon's former home. As you tour the museum's exhibits, you'll learn about Bob Marley's incredible life and career through memorabilia, photographs, and personal items. Immerse yourself in the beats of reggae music and discover the cultural significance of Jamaica's most famous musical export.

Devon House: Travel back in time with a visit to Devon House, a magnificently restored estate that celebrates Jamaica's colonial history. Devon House, built in the nineteenth century, is well-known for its exquisite Georgian architecture, rich grounds, and antique furniture. Explore the ancient halls and galleries before indulging in some of Jamaica's best ice cream at the Devon House I Scream parlor, which serves a variety of flavors inspired by local fruits and spices.

Emancipation Park: Take a leisurely stroll through Emancipation Park, a peaceful oasis in the middle of Kingston. Admire the park's lush vegetation, serene ponds, and eye-catching sculptures, including the famed "Redemption Song" monument, which commemorates Jamaica's path to freedom and independence. Relax on the lawns, soak up the sun, and enjoy the sense of calm and tranquility that pervades this urban oasis.

National Gallery of Jamaica: A visit to Jamaica's finest art institution, the National Gallery of Jamaica, will immerse you in the country's rich artistic past. Discover masterpieces by renowned artists such as Edna Manley, Albert Huie, and Barrington Watson among an extraordinary collection of Jamaican art ranging from the Taino period to modern works. The exhibition provides a complete overview of Jamaica's diversified cultural scene, including classic paintings and sculptures as well as avant-garde installations.

Port Royal: End your day excursion with a visit to Port Royal, a historic port city nicknamed the "Wickedest City on Earth" in the 17th century. Explore the relics of this once-thriving pirate refuge, such as Fort Charles, the Giddy House, and the Museum of Port Royal, which provide insight into the city's renowned history and maritime legacy. Walk in the footsteps of pirates and buccaneers as you discover the secrets and stories of Port Royal's fascinating past.

A day trip to Kingston promises a riveting blend of history, culture, and urban charm, giving visitors a better knowledge of Jamaica's past, present, and future.

Blue Mountain Excursion

Take a memorable journey to Jamaica's spectacular Blue Mountains, home to the country's highest peak and some of the most breathtaking landscapes in the Caribbean. A Blue

Mountains expedition guarantees a day of excitement, exploration, and natural beauty:

Blue Mountain Peak Hike: Put on your hiking boots and reach the summit of Blue Mountain Peak, Jamaica's highest point at 7,402 feet (2,256 meters) above sea level. Ascend to the summit via a tough but rewarding journey through lush rainforests, gushing waterfalls, and mist-shrouded summits. At the top, take in panoramic views of the island below, including the beautiful seas of the Caribbean Sea and the verdant valleys that stretch to the horizon.

Coffee Plantation Tour: Take a tour of a local coffee plantation to learn the secrets of Jamaica's world-renowned Blue Mountain Coffee. Learn about the entire coffee-growing process, from bean to cup, as trained guides take you around the plantation's fields, processing facilities, and tasting rooms. Try freshly brewed Blue Mountain Coffee and enjoy its smooth, rich flavor profile with hints of chocolate, caramel, and lemon. Learn about the history and culture of Jamaican coffee manufacturing, as well as its economic and environmental implications.

Catherine's Peak: Discover the lush landscapes and picturesque views of Catherine's Peak, a verdant mountain range in the Blue Mountains. Take a leisurely trek or beautiful drive over winding mountain roads, stopping to observe the breathtaking views and diverse flora and wildlife that survive in this untouched wilderness. Keep a look out for native birds like the Jamaican swallowtail hummingbird and the yellow-billed parrot, which live in the Blue Mountains.

Waterfalls and Rivers: Cool off from the mountain's embrace by taking a refreshing plunge in one of the Blue Mountains' many waterfalls and rivers. Dive into the crystal-clear waters of secret pools and natural springs, surrounded by lush greenery and towering bamboo trees. Listen to the calming sounds of flowing waterfalls as you unwind and revitalize in the quiet splendor of the highlands.

A Blue Mountains adventure provides an unprecedented opportunity to connect with nature, explore varied ecosystems, and see the spectacular splendor of Jamaica's mountainous interior.

Port Antonio Tour

Explore the tranquil coastal village of Port Antonio, a hidden treasure on Jamaica's northeastern coast. Port Antonio's quiet environment, lovely beaches, and lush scenery make it an ideal destination for a day trip or excursion from Ocho Rios. Here's what you'll encounter on your Port Antonio tour:

Frenchman's Cove: Start your exploration of Port Antonio with a trip to Frenchman's Cove, a quiet haven noted for its turquoise waters, pure white dunes, and lush vegetation.

Nestled between green cliffs, this natural beach provides a peaceful refuge away from the throng, where you may swim in the calm waters, relax on the smooth sands, or explore the nearby jungle paths. Take in the spectacular splendor of Frenchman's Cove, where the river and sea meet to provide a gorgeous scene reminiscent of paradise.

Blue Lagoon: Discover the alluring charm of the Blue Lagoon, a natural wonder known for its hypnotic blue hues and tranquil atmosphere. Take a boat trip across the lagoon's calm waters, where the colors change from turquoise to azure, providing a stunning show of color. Dive into the lagoon's crystal-clear depths, where mineral springs and underwater tunnels contribute to the surreal atmosphere. Take a snorkeling or glass-bottom boat excursion to see the abundant marine life and coral reefs that thrive beneath the surface, or simply relax on the beach and take in the tranquil calm of this iconic lagoon.

Reach Falls: Head inland to Reach Falls, a secluded paradise tucked in the lush jungles of Jamaica's eastern slopes. Follow winding trails through dense vegetation to find a succession of flowing waterfalls, natural pools, and emerald-green grottos hidden in the jungle. Wade through cool waters, discover hidden caverns and rock formations, and admire the natural splendor of this unspoiled paradise. Take a guided tour to learn about the indigenous plants and creatures that live at Reach Falls, and then relax in the serene atmosphere of this stunning natural beauty.

Rio Grande Rafting: Finish your Port Antonio trip with a relaxing rafting adventure down the picturesque Rio Grande River. Board a traditional bamboo raft and float downstream, surrounded by towering bamboo groves, tropical vegetation, and tumbling waterfalls. Drift down the serene waters while your skilled raft captain guides you through the moderate currents, telling you stories and legends about the river's history and tradition. Experience the tranquil beauty of the Rio Grande Valley, where lush landscapes and calm rivers provide a serene backdrop for a wonderful tour through Jamaica's natural beauties.

A Port Antonio tour provides a calm getaway into Jamaica's natural splendor, where pristine beaches, lush rainforests, and serene rivers come together to provide a unique experience in the heart of the Caribbean.

Chapter 13

WELLNESS & SPA RETREATS IN OCHO RIOS.

Escape the rush and bustle of everyday life and embark on a rejuvenating and relaxing visit to Ocho Rios. Nestled along Jamaica's gorgeous coastline, Ocho Rios provides a peaceful haven for those seeking wellness and tranquillity. From opulent spa resorts to holistic healing techniques, this chapter delves into the wide range of health and spa retreats available in Ocho Rios.

Spa Resorts and Wellness Centres

Indulge your senses and rejuvenate your body and mind at Ocho Rios' luxury spa resorts and wellness facilities. From relaxing massages to revitalizing treatments, these sanctuaries of relaxation provide a pleasant respite from the worries of daily life:

Sandals Ochi Beach Resort: Immerse yourself in luxury at Sandals Ochi Beach Resort, where the Red Lane Spa welcomes you with a menu of luxurious treatments inspired by the natural beauty of the Caribbean. A deep tissue massage, a relaxing hydrotherapy pool, or a nutritious body scrub can all help you feel better. The Red Lane Spa, with its tranquil setting and professional therapists, offers a haven for relaxation and regeneration.

Moon Palace Jamaica: At Moon Palace Jamaica, you can experience the utmost in wellness and elegance, including the sumptuous Awe Spa. Choose from a wide range of therapeutic massages, facials, and body treatments that will relax and restore your body. Indulge in the restorative properties of local ingredients like aloe vera, coconut, and coffee, or choose a custom spa package that combines various treatments for a fully immersive experience.

Jewel Paradise Cove Resort & Spa: Experience paradise at Jewel Paradise Cove Resort & Spa, where the Radiant Spa provides a comprehensive approach to wellness and relaxation. Relax in the steam room, sauna, or whirlpool before receiving a personalized massage or body treatment based on your specific needs. From aromatherapy to reflexology, the Radiant Spa offers a haven for healing and restoration, allowing you to disconnect from the worries of everyday life and reconnect with your inner calm.

Ocean Spa: Located on the cliffs overlooking the Caribbean Sea, Ocean Spa provides a peaceful refuge where nature and wellness meet. Immerse yourself in the calming sounds of the ocean as experienced therapists provide you with a selection of revitalizing treatments such as hot stone massages, coconut scrubs, and seaweed wraps. Relax in the outdoor hydrotherapy pool, surrounded by beautiful tropical gardens and breathtaking ocean views, allowing nature's therapeutic forces to restore balance to your body and spirit.

Tropical Bliss Spa: Tropical Bliss Spa offers the ideal relaxing experience, combining traditional Jamaican hospitality with world-class wellness treatments. Choose from a variety of massages, facials, and body treatments that encourage relaxation, renewal, and overall recovery. From Swedish massage to aromatherapy, each treatment is tailored to your specific needs, resulting in a personalized experience that will leave you feeling refreshed, invigorated, and revived.

Ocho Rios' spa resorts and wellness centers provide a refuge of peace and refreshment, combining experienced therapists and exquisite amenities to create an amazing wellness experience.

Holistic Healing Practices.

Discover the ancient art of holistic treatment in Ocho Rios, where traditional Jamaican cures and modern health methods come together to promote physical, mental, and spiritual well-being. From herbal medicines to energy therapy, explore the varied range of holistic health techniques offered in Ocho Rios:

Herbal Medicine: Learn about Jamaica's rich herbal traditions by visiting a local pharmacy or herbalist and discovering the medicinal benefits of indigenous herbs and botanicals. Learn about the medicinal properties of herbs like ginger, turmeric, and moringa, which have been used for millennia to cure a wide range of diseases and boost general health. Whether you're looking for relief from stress, pain, or digestive disorders, herbal medicine provides a natural and comprehensive approach to healing that respects nature's wisdom.

Aromatherapy: With aromatherapy, you may immerse yourself in the healing power of fragrance. This therapeutic technique harnesses the fragrant essences of plant extracts to promote relaxation and harmony. Experience the relaxing benefits of essential oils like lavender, eucalyptus, and chamomile, which may help reduce stress, improve sleep quality, and improve overall health. Give yourself an aromatherapy massage or take a fragrant steam bath, and allow the transformational fragrances transport you to a state of profound rest and tranquillity.

Energy Healing: Discover the ancient technique of energy healing, which aims to restore balance and harmony to the body's energy centers, or chakras. Discover Reiki, a Japanese type of energy healing that uses universal life force energy to promote healing and relaxation. Alternatively, look into crystal therapy, which uses the therapeutic powers of crystals and gemstones to cleanse, balance, and align the body's energy systems. Whether you select Reiki, crystal treatment, or another type of energy healing, you'll feel a deep feeling of calm and regeneration as stagnant energy is released and vitality is restored.

Sound Therapy: Immerse yourself in the relaxing sounds of nature with sound therapy, a healing method that uses sound vibrations to induce relaxation, decrease stress, and improve overall well-being. Tibetan singing bowls, crystal bowls, and tuning forks produce harmonic vibrations that vibrate throughout your body and mind, alleviating tension and restoring equilibrium. Sound therapy can be experienced in individual sessions, group seminars, or immersion sound baths, in which participants lie back and let the therapeutic vibrations to wash over them, resulting in great relaxation and inner calm.

Meditation and awareness: With meditation, you may cultivate awareness and inner calm while also promoting relaxation, clarity, and emotional well-being. Take part in guided meditation classes conducted by expert teachers, who will gently guide you through methods like breath awareness, body scanning, and loving-kindness meditation. Alternatively, try mindfulness activities like walking meditation, mindful eating, or nature meditation, which promote present-moment awareness and connection to the environment around you. Whether you're a novice or an experienced meditator, Ocho Rios provides a range of chances to practice meditation and mindfulness in a friendly and compassionate setting.

Holistic healing techniques in Ocho Rios provide a comprehensive approach to wellbeing, combining ancient knowledge, current science, and nature's healing power to create balance, harmony, and energy in mind, body, and spirit.

Yoga and Meditation Retreats.

Yoga and meditation retreats in Ocho Rios, nestled among the lush landscapes and quiet coasts, provide a chance for searchers of inner peace and holistic wellbeing to refresh mind, body, and soul. Going on a retreat in Ocho Rios not only gives you a break from the everyday grind, but it also allows you to find yourself and evolve. Here's what you can expect from attending yoga and meditation retreats in Ocho Rios.

Everyday Yoga classes: Awaken your body and mind with vigorous yoga classes held everyday in the tranquil setting of Ocho Rios. These workshops, led by experienced yoga instructors, are open to practitioners of all skill levels, from beginners to expert yogis. Practice a range of yoga types, such as Hatha, Vinyasa, Yin, and Ashtanga, each with their own set of advantages for physical strength, flexibility, and mental clarity. Whether you prefer the smooth flow of morning yoga on the beach or the contemplative silence of nighttime restorative yoga, Ocho Rios retreats provide a variety of chances to enhance your practice and learn new methods.

Meditation and Mindfulness Practices: Ocho Rios' yoga retreats include guided meditation and mindfulness workshops to help you cultivate inner serenity and presence. Explore ancient meditation practices that promote relaxation, stress reduction, and emotional well-being, such as mindfulness, loving-kindness, and breath awareness. As you immerse yourself in the transformational power of meditation in the calm natural settings of Ocho Rios, you will learn to quiet the oscillations of your mind and connect with your true nature.

Workshops & Seminars: Gain a better grasp of yoga philosophy, anatomy, and holistic wellbeing via engaging workshops and seminars taught by expert instructors and guest speakers. Explore Ayurveda, the chakra system, and the science of mindfulness to acquire insights that can help you strengthen your practice and broaden your awareness. Participate in talks, group activities, and experiential learning opportunities that will help you incorporate yoga and mindfulness into your everyday life, promoting overall well-being and personal growth.

Nature Immersion and Outdoor Activities: Take advantage of Ocho Rios' natural splendor by participating in nature-based excursions and activities that complement your yoga and meditation practice. Take guided treks through lush jungles, swim in isolated waterfalls, or practice yoga on gorgeous beaches to connect with nature and awaken your senses. Experience nature's transformational power while deepening your respect for the interdependence of all living beings and cultivating a feeling of peace with your surroundings.

Nutritious Cuisine & Wellness Meals: During your yoga retreat in Ocho Rios, nourish your body and spirit with nourishing, plant-based cuisine that supports your wellness journey. Indulge in delectable meals made with locally sourced products that are packed with brilliant flavors and wholesome minerals. Each meal, from fresh tropical fruits and robust salads to nutritious soups and revitalizing smoothies, is carefully designed to fuel your body, boost energy, and support your overall well-being.

Community and Connection: Make significant relationships and create a sense of community with others who share your enthusiasm for yoga, meditation, and holistic living. Participate in group discussions, share experiences, and celebrate your path of self-discovery and growth in a safe and friendly atmosphere. Cultivate connections and long-term ties that will enhance your life with love, humor, and knowledge.

Participating in a yoga and meditation retreat in Ocho Rios provides an incredible chance for self-discovery, healing, and rejuvenation, allowing you to experience the transformational power of mindfulness, movement, and mindful living in the beautiful splendor of Jamaica's tropical paradise.

Chapter 14

ITINERARY AND SAMPLE PLANS

Planning a vacation to Ocho Rios may be both thrilling and overwhelming, especially because there are so many sights and activities to do.

In this chapter, we'll provide you some example itineraries and plans to help you make the most of your stay in Ocho Rios, whether you're searching for a peaceful weekend trip or a deep dive into local culture.

Weekend Getaway

A weekend trip allows you to escape the hustle and bustle of daily life and immerse yourself in Ocho Rios' natural beauty and colorful culture. With careful preparation and clever selections, you may see the most of this tropical paradise in only a few days. Here is an example schedule for a fantastic weekend in Ocho Rios.

Day One: Arrival and Beach Day.

Morning: Arrive at Ocho Rios and settle into your accommodations. Begin your day with a leisurely breakfast at a nearby café or restaurant, preparing for the adventures ahead.

Late morning: Visit one of Ocho Rios' exquisite beaches, such as Turtle Beach or Mahogany Beach, to soak up the sun and relax on the soft sands. Take a relaxing plunge in the turquoise waters of the Caribbean Sea and participate in water sports such as snorkeling or kayaking.

Afternoon: Have a fantastic meal at a beachside restaurant, relishing fresh seafood dishes and tropical beverages while admiring panoramic views of the coast.

Late afternoon: Stroll around Ocho Rios' bustling streets, stopping at stores and markets for souvenirs and local crafts. The Ocho Rios Craft Market is a must-see for anybody looking for handcrafted jewelry, artwork, and other one-of-a-kind items.

Evening: Enjoy a delicious supper at a beachfront restaurant, with Jamaican classics such as jerk chicken, ackee and saltfish, and fried plantains. End the evening with a romantic stroll down the beach, watching the sun set over the horizon.

Day two: Adventure & Exploration.

Morning: Get up early and go on an exciting excursion to Dunn's River Falls, one of Jamaica's most famous natural attractions. Join a guided trip to ascend the flowing waterfalls and navigate the limestone terraces and natural pools with the assistance of expert guides. Take pauses to swim and splash in the cool waters, surrounded by beautiful tropical foliage.

Late Morning: After descending from Dunn's River Falls, visit surrounding sites including Mystic Mountain. Riding the Sky Explorer chairlift into the rainforest canopy provides panoramic views of Ocho Rios and the surrounding scenery. Consider extra activities such as ziplining, bobsledding, or touring the butterfly and hummingbird gardens.

Afternoon: Refuel with a delicious lunch at a local restaurant, where you may sample both Jamaican and foreign food. Take some time to rest and unwind at your hotel, possibly with a spa treatment or by the pool.

Evening: Go out for an evening of fun and feasting. Choose from a range of alternatives, including live music venues, seaside pubs, and cultural shows. Dance the night away to the sounds of reggae music or spend a relaxing evening beneath the sky.

Day Three: Cultural exploration and departure.

Early Morning: Begin your day by visiting the Bob Marley Museum in neighboring Kingston. Explore the iconic reggae musician's old home and recording studio to learn about his life, music, and legacy. Explore the museum's exhibitions, which include memorabilia, pictures, and personal objects belonging to Bob Marley.

Late Morning: Dine at a local restaurant for a typical Jamaican breakfast, which includes ackee and saltfish, callaloo, and fried dumplings.

Afternoon: Return to Ocho Rios and immerse yourself in local culture by visiting the Harmony Hall Art Gallery. Discover modern Jamaican artwork, sculptures, and crafts produced by local artists, as well as one-of-a-kind souvenirs and presents for sale.

Evening: Say goodbye to Ocho Rios and go for your next destination, carrying with you memories of memorable experiences and adventures in this tropical paradise.

This example itinerary showcases the best that Ocho Rios has to offer, blending leisure, adventure, and cultural discovery for an unforgettable weekend trip.

Cultural Immersion

In Ocho Rios, you may embark on a voyage of cultural discovery and immersion as you witness the rich tapestry of Jamaican tradition emerge before you. Explore the island's unique cultural landscape, delving deeply into its history, customs, and creative expression. Below is a planned agenda for an interesting cultural immersion experience in Ocho Rios:

Day One: Arrival and Historical Exploration

Morning: Arrive at Ocho Rios and check into your accommodations. Begin your cultural immersion experience with a visit to Seville Heritage Park and Museum. Explore the relics of the 16th-century Spanish settlement, wander through the Taino village replica, and participate in interactive displays celebrating Jamaica's indigenous heritage.

Late morning: Continue your history journey by visiting the Columbus Park Museum. Discover artifacts and displays depicting the interactions between indigenous peoples and European explorers, including Christopher Columbus. Learn about Jamaica's colonial history and how it shaped the island's cultural identity.

Afternoon: Enjoy a classic Jamaican meal at a neighborhood restaurant, with genuine foods such as jerk chicken, rice and peas, and fried plantains.

Late afternoon: Visit the historic Rio Nuevo Battle Site, where English and Spanish armies fought for sovereignty of Jamaica in the 17th century. Explore the museum's displays, artifacts, and archaeological finds to learn about the key events that formed the island's colonial history.

Evening: Spend a relaxing evening in Ocho Rios, wandering along the waterfront promenade or dining at a beachfront restaurant where you can sample fresh seafood while taking in the island atmosphere.

Day two: Cultural heritage and artistic expression.

Morning cultural tour to Firefly Estate, former home of Sir Noël Coward, a famous playwright and entertainer. Explore the estate's gardens, which sit on a hill overlooking the Caribbean Sea and provide panoramic views of the coastline. Learn about Coward's contributions to Jamaican arts and culture, as well as his lasting impact.

Late morning: Take in the lush surroundings of Turtle River Falls and Gardens, a botanical sanctuary in the heart of Ocho Rios. Wander through tropical gardens, see flowing waterfalls, and see local flora and wildlife. Participate in guided excursions highlighting Jamaica's natural beauty and biological variety.

Afternoon: Explore the local art scene with a trip to Island Village, a cultural hotspot that showcases Jamaican craftsmanship and innovation. Visit artisanal stores, galleries, and studios to examine and purchase handcrafted artworks, ceramics, and jewelry. Engage with local artists and craftspeople, learning about their creative processes and inspirations.

Late afternoon: Join a cultural class or presentation to learn traditional Jamaican skills like basket weaving, batik printing, or drumming. Participate in hands-on activities that highlight the island's creative legacy and encourage cultural interchange.

Evening: Finish your cultural immersion with a meal at a local restaurant that includes live music and entertainment. Immerse yourself in the beats of reggae, ska, and dancehall while celebrating Jamaica's diverse musical traditions and artistic expression.

Day Three: Culinary exploration and departure.

Morning: Take a gastronomic tour of Ocho Rios, including local markets, spice shops, and street food booths. Engage with vendors, sample exotic fruits and spices, and discover the many flavors and ingredients that constitute Jamaican cuisine.

Late Morning: Take a cooking lesson or culinary tour to learn traditional Jamaican foods and methods from renowned chefs. Prepare and enjoy meals such as jerk chicken, curry goat, and festival while learning about the unique combination of African, European, and Indigenous influences that create Jamaican cuisine.

Afternoon: Reflect on your cultural experiences while enjoying a goodbye lunch at a beachside restaurant, relishing the tastes of Jamaica for the last time. Share tales and memories with other travelers, and celebrate the friendships formed through shared adventure and discovery.

Departure: Say goodbye to Ocho Rios and travel for your next destination with a renewed respect for Jamaica's rich cultural heritage and creative legacy. Carry with you the memories, insights, and ideas garnered from your cultural immersion experience, knowing that the spirit of Jamaica will live on in your heart and soul.

Outdoor Adventure

Ocho Rios is more than simply a relaxing destination; it's also a mecca for outdoor explorers looking for adrenaline-pumping activities and magnificent natural scenery. From exploring beautiful jungles to engaging on exhilarating water-based excursions, Ocho Rios has a plethora of outdoor attractions for both nature enthusiasts and adrenaline seekers. Here's a full look at outdoor adventure activities in Ocho Rios:

Rainforest Hiking Trails.

Take a journey into Ocho Rios' lush jungles, where towering trees, flowing waterfalls, and varied species await. Lace up your hiking boots and enjoy the following popular hiking trails:

Blue Mountain Peak Trail: Test your limits by hiking to the peak of Jamaica's highest point, Blue Mountain Peak. Navigate challenging terrain and rich foliage as you travel through mist-shrouded woods and cloud-covered summits. Admire panoramic views of the island below and experience spectacular sunrises and sunsets from the peak.

Coyaba River Garden and Museum: Experience the serene beauty of Coyaba River Garden, a floral wonderland located in the center of Ocho Rios. Wander down shady paths adorned with exotic flora and wildlife, such as tropical flowers, ferns, and fruit trees. Explore the museum's artifacts and exhibitions, which highlight Jamaica's diverse cultural heritage and indigenous history.

Turtle River Falls & Gardens: Immerse yourself in the natural beauty of Turtle River Falls and Gardens, a peaceful haven only minutes from Ocho Rios' bustling town center. Follow meandering paths through lush gardens, past flowing waterfalls, and across scenic bridges. As you explore this gorgeous refuge, you'll discover secret grottos, bathe in cold natural pools, and see native birds and fauna.

Zipline and Canopy Tours

Soar through the trees and feel the rush of ziplining and canopy excursions in Ocho Rios' beautiful jungles. Strap into a harness, take a deep breath, and ready for a thrilling journey as you zip between platforms high above the forest floor. Here are some of the best zipline and canopy tour experiences in Ocho Rios:

Mystic Mountain: Experience a high-flying experience at Mystic Mountain, home of Jamaica's top zipline and canopy tour. Fly through the canopy at high speeds, skimming over lush valleys and glittering streams. Take in panoramic vistas of the jungle below and experience a sense of excitement as you navigate twists, turns, and hair-raising descents.

Chukka Caribbean Adventures: Experience the excitement of ziplining and canopy excursions with Chukka Caribbean Adventures, which provides a range of adrenaline-pumping activities in Ocho Rios. Choose from zip lines that go across mountainous terrain, suspension bridges that wobble in the breeze, and treetop platforms that provide bird's-eye views of the rainforest canopy.

ATV and Jeep Safari Excursions

Explore Ocho Rios' rough terrain and stunning sceneries with thrilling ATV and Jeep safari adventures. Climb on an all-terrain vehicle or rugged jeep and go off on off-road adventures through Jamaica's unspoiled nature. Here are several must-experience ATV and Jeep safari adventures in Ocho Rios:

Yaaman Adventure Park: Prepare for an adrenaline-fueled ride through Yaaman Adventure Park, where ATV and Jeep safari trips provide exhilarating adventures for explorers of all ages. As you explore the park's different environments, you'll see lush woods, muddy pathways, and rocky terrain. Keep a look out for natural species, which includes unusual birds, reptiles, and animals that live in the park.

Dunn's River Falls ATV Safari: Combine adventure and natural beauty on the Dunn's River Falls ATV Safari, a guided excursion that takes you off the main road and deep into Jamaica's countryside. Ride through tropical woods, banana fields, and rural communities while learning about the island's history, culture, and environment. Finish up your tour with a relaxing swim at the famed Dunn's River Falls, where cascading waters provide a revitalizing experience amidst stunning landscape.

Family-friendly trip.

Ocho Rios welcomes families with a variety of attractions and activities designed to engage both children and adults. From visiting natural reserves to splashing in crystal-clear seas, Ocho Rios is a great location for families to make treasured experiences together. Here's a comprehensive guide to organizing a wonderful family trip to Ocho Rios:

Turtle River Park

Begin your family adventure with a visit to Turtle River Park, an attractive green spot hidden in Ocho Rios. Wander along meandering routes surrounded by lush foliage and beautiful water features. The park has a playground for children to play on, as well as picnic areas where families may enjoy a meal in the tranquility of nature.

Horseback Riding Tours

Take an equine journey through Ocho Rios' stunning scenery. Ride horseback over sandy beaches and woodland pathways, allowing the entire family to interact with nature in an unforgettable way. Choose from guided excursions tailored to different ability levels, assuring a safe and entertaining experience for all.

Family-Friendly Beaches.

Ocho Rios boasts beautiful beaches perfect for families looking for sun-soaked leisure and aquatic adventure. Turtle Beach and Mahogany Beach are family favorites, with calm waves and soft beaches ideal for building sandcastles and playing beach activities. Allow the youngsters to swim in the calm surf as the parents relax under the Caribbean sun.

Dolphin Cove

Dolphin Cove offers families the opportunity to interact with dolphins, swim among stingrays, and enjoy exotic birds. Enjoy the antics of cheerful dolphins as they do acrobatics and demonstrate their intellect. Dolphin Cove is a must-see for families.

Rainforest Adventure

Venture into the heart of Jamaica's beautiful jungles for an excursion that the entire family will enjoy. Glide over Mystic Mountain's lush canopy in a gondola, taking in spectacular views of the surrounding regions. Thrill-seekers may take a bobsled ride or zip line under the forest canopy, while nature lovers can visit botanical gardens and nature paths.

Cultural Experiences.

Immerse your family in Jamaica's unique culture via exciting activities and experiences. Visit the Bob Marley Museum in

Kingston to learn about the reggae icon's life and legacy. Explore local markets and artisan stores to get handcrafted items and learn about the island's creative heritage.

Adventure Parks

Experience adrenaline-pumping thrills at Ocho Rios' adventure parks, where families may push their limits on thrilling rides and attractions. Mystic Mountain has a variety of activities, such as ziplining, bobsledding, and nature paths. Chukka Caribbean Adventures offers thrilling activities such as river tubing and dune buggy rides for an action-packed family day.

Interactive Wildlife Encounters

Experience Jamaica's unique wildlife through participatory activities at wildlife reserves and sanctuaries. Explore the calm settings of Konoko Falls and Gardens, which are home to unique flora and animals, including indigenous Jamaican species. Learn about conservation efforts and engage with friendly animals to provide a memorable experience for the entire family.

Family Friendly Dining

Taste the flavors of Jamaica at family-friendly restaurants that serve a range of gastronomic pleasures. Indulge on Jamaican staples such as jerk chicken, festival, and rice and peas, while children may enjoy traditional favorites with a Caribbean twist. Many restaurants include kid-friendly menus and outside seating, allowing families to dine in comfort while taking in the scenery.

Embark on a family journey to Ocho Rios and make memorable experiences amid the island's natural beauty, cultural diversity, and friendly people. Ocho Rios offers a variety of family-friendly attractions and activities, ensuring an amazing holiday for families looking for fun, relaxation, and adventure.

Budget Travel

Traveling to Ocho Rios on a budget does not imply compromising quality or skipping out on unforgettable experiences. With careful planning and wise decisions, you may visit this Caribbean jewel without breaking the budget. Here's a thorough guide to budget tourism in Ocho Rios, including inexpensive lodgings and budget-friendly activities:

Accommodation Options.

Hostels and Guesthouses: Ocho Rios has a number of low-cost lodgings, including hostels and guesthouses, where you may find pleasant housing at reasonable rates. Choose dormitory-style or private rooms with shared utilities to save money while still enjoying convenient locations and basic amenities.

Budget Hotels: Look for budget hotels and motels in Ocho Rios that provide clean and comfortable rooms at reasonable prices. Many cheap hotels offer important facilities like air conditioning, Wi-Fi, and free breakfast, guaranteeing a comfortable stay without breaking the bank.

Holiday Rentals: If you're going with a party or family, think about renting an affordable apartment or holiday home in Ocho Rios. Vacation rentals provide the comfort of home-like amenities like as kitchens and living rooms, allowing you to save money on dining out while still having a more real travel experience.

Dining On a Budget

Local Eateries and Street Food: Sample Ocho Rios' gastronomic scene by visiting cheap local restaurants and street food sellers. Enjoy Jamaican staples such as jerk chicken, patties, and seafood meals at reasonable costs. Look for roadside booths and food markets where you may enjoy authentic cuisines without spending a fortune.

Cook Your Own Meals: Save money on dining out by making your own meals with fresh products from local markets and stores. Many lodgings have kitchen facilities or community kitchens where you may prepare homemade meals and enjoy low-cost eating alternatives throughout your stay.

Transportation Tips.

Public Transportation: Use Ocho Rios' public transportation system, which includes buses and minibuses, to tour the city and adjacent attractions at a low fee. Public buses are an inexpensive way to move around town, while minibuses provide easy access to important tourist attractions and landmarks.

Walking and Cycling: Explore Ocho Rios on foot or by bicycle to save money on transportation while also experiencing the city's colorful ambiance up close. Many sights and areas of interest are within walking distance of one another, enabling you to explore at your own speed while discovering hidden treasures along the way.

Free and Low-Cost Activities.

Beach hopping: Spend lazy days soaking up the sun and swimming on Ocho Rios' magnificent beaches, many of which are free to use and provide breathtaking views of the Caribbean Sea. Pack a lunch, bring your beach blanket, and spend the day relaxing without paying a dollar.

Nature Trails and Parks: Discover Ocho Rios' natural splendor by taking picturesque treks and nature walks via nearby parks and reserves. Visit sights such as Turtle River Falls and Gardens or trek to the top of Dunn's River Falls for unique natural experiences at a low cost.

Cultural Immersion: Discover Jamaican culture and tradition by visiting local markets, attending cultural events, and seeing historical monuments and museums. Many cultural activities and events are free or low-cost, allowing visitors to interact with locals while learning about the island's rich history and traditions.

Shop Smart

Bargain Hunting: Visit Ocho Rios' artisan markets and retail areas to get great deals on souvenirs, handicrafts, and local items. Improve your negotiating abilities and barter with sellers to get the greatest discounts on unique presents and souvenirs to remember your trip by.

Shop off the Beaten Path: Visit lesser-known shopping neighborhoods and boutique businesses in Ocho Rios to find hidden jewels and locally crafted goods at reasonable costs. Avoid tourist traps and high-end boutiques, and instead look for real Jamaican items and souvenirs sold by individual artists and craftspeople.

Solo Traveler's Guide

Taking a single trip to Ocho Rios gives up new possibilities for adventure, self-discovery, and cultural immersion. As a single traveler, you may explore at your own speed, pursue particular interests, and form important connections with locals and other travelers. Here's a complete guide to assist solo explorers navigate Ocho Rios confidently and enthusiastically:

Embrace Independence

Mindful Planning: Before leaving, do extensive study on Ocho Rios' attractions, transportation alternatives, and safety precautions. Familiarize yourself with the local culture, customs, and language so you can explore the destination with confidence and respect.

Pack Smart: Travel light and bring necessities like a dependable map or navigation software, sunscreen, bug repellant, a reusable water bottle, and good walking shoes. Consider taking a portable charger to keep your electronics charged during your trips.

Safety & Security

Stay Informed: Learn about current safety advice and local legislation in Ocho Rios. Save emergency contacts, including the local embassy or consulate, to your phone, and save copies of crucial papers like your passport and travel insurance.

Trust Your Instincts: Use cautious, especially in unexpected situations. Avoid secluded regions, particularly after dark, and remain aware of your surroundings at all times. Consider selecting trustworthy transportation and lodging options suggested by other tourists.

Accommodation Choices

Lone-Friendly lodgings: Select lodgings that appeal to lone travelers, such as hostels, guesthouses, and boutique hotels. These places frequently have common areas where you may connect with other tourists, swap travel advice, and make new acquaintances.

Safety and Comfort: Prioritize safety and comfort when choosing housing choices. Look for well rated accommodations with safe locks, 24-hour reception, and favorable reviews from single travelers. Consider selecting rooms in strategic locations to ensure easy access to activities and facilities.

Cultural Immersion.

Engage with Locals: Take advantage of opportunities to interact with Jamaicans and learn about their culture. Start conversations with shops, street sellers, and locals to learn about their everyday lives, customs, and viewpoints. Respect local customs and manners to establish lasting friendships.

Attend Cultural Events: Keep an eye out for cultural events, festivals, and festivities in Ocho Rios. Participate in music performances, art displays, and culinary experiences to learn about Jamaica's rich cultural legacy and artistic expression.

Exploring Solo.

Self-Guided Exploration: Travel at your own leisure through Ocho Rios, seeking for hidden treasures and real encounters. Wander through crowded marketplaces, scenic beaches, and ancient districts to discover the city's many attractions.

Participate in Group Activities: Join group tours, excursions, and activities to experience Ocho Rios' highlights and socialize with other tourists. Joining hiking trips, snorkeling tours, or cultural strolling tours allows you to share experiences and make memorable memories with other travelers.

Dining Solo

Local Cuisine: Sample Jamaica's wonderful cuisine at restaurants, food markets, and on the street. Accept the opportunity to dine alone, enjoying delectable delicacies like jerk chicken, ackee and saltfish, and fresh seafood meals.

Community Dining: Participate in communal dining experiences or culinary tours to meet locals and other visitors while sharing meals and discussion. Participate in culinary exchanges, sampling regional specialties and sharing experiences and suggestions with newfound acquaintances.

Stay connected.

Digital Nomad Resources: Use digital nomad resources like coworking spaces, internet cafés, and Wi-Fi hotspots to stay connected and productive on your solo excursions in Ocho Rios. Maintain connection with friends and family using social media, messaging apps, and email to share updates and remain in touch across distances.

Solo travel to Ocho Rios provides opportunities for personal development, cultural enrichment, and amazing adventures. Accept the voyage with an open heart and an adventurous attitude, enjoying the beauty and diversity of Jamaica's stunning landscapes and dynamic towns.

Romantic Getaways in Ocho Rios.

Ocho Rios, with its stunning surroundings, clean beaches, and romantic environment, is an ideal place for couples looking for an unforgettable romantic holiday. From quiet seaside meals to exhilarating treks through beautiful jungles, Ocho Rios has a multitude of enticing options for lovebirds. Here's a complete guide on organizing the ideal romantic getaway in Ocho Rios:

Choosing the Perfect Accommodation.

Luxury Resorts: For the ultimate romantic vacation, plan a stay at one of Ocho Rios' finest resorts. Choose from world-class resorts like Sandals Royal Plantation, Couples Tower Isle, and Moon Palace Jamaica Grande, which provide lavish rooms, customized service, and breathtaking ocean views.

Boutique Hotels and Villas: For a more private and personalized romantic getaway, choose tiny boutique hotels or private villas tucked along Ocho Rios' shoreline. Enjoy solitude, quiet, and breathtaking views of the Caribbean Sea while indulging in the comforts of home in a luxury environment.

Overwater Bungalows: For an unforgettable romantic experience, stay in an overwater bungalow at Sandals South Coast or Sandals Royal Caribbean. Drift off to sleep to the calming sounds of the surf, eat breakfast on your private patio, and soak up the splendor of crystal-clear seas only feet from your door.

Romantic Dinner Experiences

Beachside Dining: Indulge your senses with a romantic beachside supper beneath the stars. Many resorts in Ocho Rios have private dining experiences on the beach, where you may enjoy gourmet meals while listening to the calm sound of waves lapping against the coast.

Fine Dining Restaurants: Discover Ocho Rios' culinary scene by dining at upmarket restaurants that serve superb food in an intimate setting. Enjoy Jamaican favorites, fresh seafood, and foreign cuisines while admiring panoramic views of the Caribbean Sea or beautiful tropical gardens.

Candlelight Dinners: Surprise your lover with a candlelight supper in a quiet garden or gazebo, providing a romantic setting and undisturbed seclusion. Many resorts and boutique hotels provide bespoke dining experiences designed to help couples make lasting memories.

Romantic Activities and Experiences

Sunset Cruises: Take a sunset boat down Ocho Rios' coastline, where you can soak in the golden hues of the Caribbean sunset while sipping champagne and listening to live music. Set sail on a catamaran or private yacht and enjoy the romance of the wide sea beside your loved one.

Private Beach Picnics: Take your lover to a quiet beach for a private picnic where you may relax in a serene atmosphere surrounded by natural beauty. Pack a gourmet basket full with delicious food, champagne, and tropical fruits, and spend precious time together basking in the sun and sea wind.

Waterfall Adventures: Go on a romantic trip to one of Ocho Rios' famous waterfalls, such as Dunn's River Falls or Blue Hole. Hold hands as you climb the cascading levels of the falls, bathe in crystal-clear pools, and enjoy the rejuvenating sensation of nature's splendor together.

Spa Retreats & Couples Treatments

Spa Escapes: Treat yourself to a refreshing spa vacation at one of Ocho Rios' luxury wellness centers. Enjoy couples massages, aromatherapy treatments, and holistic rituals that will soothe your mind, body, and soul. Allow experienced therapists to cure you and leave feeling rejuvenated and invigorated.

Private Spa Experiences: Treat yourself to a private spa experience in the privacy of your own home. Many resorts and boutique hotels have in-room spa services, allowing you to get individualized treatments and pampering without leaving the comfort of your romantic retreat.

Adventure & Exploration

Rainforest Romance: Go on a romantic trip through Ocho Rios' lush jungles, hiking along gorgeous routes, exploring secret waterfalls, and seeing exotic species together. Take a leisurely stroll through botanical gardens, fly through the canopy, or have a romantic picnic surrounded by nature's beauty.

Island Excursions: With a bespoke tour suited to your interests, you may explore the beauty of Ocho Rios and the neighboring islands. Charter a boat for a day of snorkeling, discover quiet coves and coral reefs, or take a helicopter trip for panoramic views of Jamaica's stunning landscapes.

Personalized Experiences.

Surprise Gestures: Surprise your sweetheart with meaningful gestures and bespoke experiences that honor your love and leave a lasting impression. Arrange for romantic turndown services, surprise champagne brunches, or private sunset yoga sessions to take your romantic holiday to the next level.

Destination Weddings and Vow Renewals: Consider Ocho Rios as the ideal location for your destination wedding or vow renewal ceremony. Exchanging vows against the background of blue lakes, lush mountains, or flowing waterfalls will provide a spectacular celebration of your love surrounded by nature's splendor.

Recording Memories

Photographic Sessions: Capture your romantic moments in Ocho Rios with professional photographic sessions that are suited to your needs. Hire a photographer to capture your travels, seashore rendezvous, and private moments, ensuring that your memories last a lifetime through breathtaking images.

Mementos & Souvenirs: Remember your romantic holiday with mementos and souvenirs that bring back memories of your time together in Ocho Rios. Shop for handcrafted crafts, local artwork, and personalized jewelry to keep as memories of your love and travels in paradise.

A romantic weekend in Ocho Rios provides beautiful experiences, poignant moments, and unique memories that will last long after your trip is over.

Chapter 15

LOCAL FESTIVALS AND EVENTS IN OCHO RIOS

Ocho Rios is well-known for its spectacular natural beauty and vibrant culture, as well as for its exciting festivals and events that highlight Jamaica's rich legacy and artistic abilities. From world-renowned music festivals to cultural gatherings commemorating local icons, Ocho Rios provides a wide range of opportunities for tourists to immerse themselves in the island's dynamic atmosphere. Here's a thorough list of the local festivals and events you won't want to miss in Ocho Rios:

Ocho Rios Jazz Festival.

The Ocho Rios Jazz Festival celebrates Jamaica's passion of music and rich jazz legacy. This famous festival, held annually in June, brings together local and international jazz performers to create an exhilarating atmosphere of musical excellence and cultural interchange. From deep saxophone solos to mesmerizing vocal performances, the Ocho Rios Jazz

Festival captivates listeners with its diverse lineup of world-class musicians and tiny settings.

Highlights from the Ocho Rios Jazz Festival:

Concerts beneath the Stars: Enjoy the wonder of live jazz concerts beneath the glittering Caribbean sky at different outdoor venues across Ocho Rios. From coastal stages to beautiful botanical gardens, each event provides a one-of-a-kind environment and musical experience.

Jam Sessions and seminars: Participate in interactive jam sessions and seminars hosted by performers and fellow jazz fans throughout the festival. Immerse yourself in the art of jazz improvisation, learn about its history, and connect with others who share your enthusiasm for music and culture.

Cultural Experiences: In addition to music, the Ocho Rios Jazz Festival highlights Jamaica's colorful culture with art exhibitions, cuisine showcases, and dance performances. Explore local markets, experience unique Jamaican food, and explore the island's artistic riches while enjoying the festival's celebratory atmosphere.

Bob Marley's Birthday Celebration

Jamaica, the birthplace of reggae music and home to iconic artist Bob Marley, honors its cultural hero with an annual birthday celebration that attracts music fans and Marley admirers from all over the world. The Bob Marley Birthday Celebration, held every February, recognizes the reggae legend's ongoing impact and musical accomplishments with a series of concerts, tributes, and cultural events.

Highlights from the Bob Marley Birthday Celebration:

Concerts & Performances: Witness the power of live reggae music as top local and international performers pay tribute to Bob Marley's renowned songs and everlasting melodies. From small acoustic sessions to spectacular stage performances, the event highlights the reggae genre's many abilities and inspirations.

Tours of Bob Marley's Home: Visit the Bob Marley Museum in Kingston to get to the core of reggae music and experience the musician's old home and recording studio. Explore Marley's life and legacy while walking through the historic site and immersing yourself in the essence of reggae culture.

Cultural Immersion: Participate in art exhibitions, film screenings, and educational events during the Bob Marley

Birthday Celebration to connect with local communities and learn about Jamaica's colorful culture. Learn about the Rastafarian movement, the origins of reggae music, and meet other admirers of Marley's music and message.

Reggae Sumfest.

Reggae Sumfest is the crown jewel of Jamaica's music festival industry, bringing thousands of music fans and revelers to Montego Bay every year for an exhilarating celebration of reggae music and Caribbean culture. This renowned event, held in July, boasts an incredible roster of reggae, dancehall, and soca musicians, providing a memorable musical, dance, and fellowship experience.

Highlights at Reggae Sumfest:

Main Stage Performances: Dance to the sounds of reggae music as top local and worldwide musicians hit the stage, delivering thrilling performances and unforgettable experiences. From iconic legends to new performers, Reggae Sumfest celebrates Jamaica's music scene and pays tribute to the genre's long history.

Sound System Showdown: Witness the throbbing intensity of Jamaican sound system culture via dramatic conflicts between rival sound systems vying for musical dominance. Feel the bass resonate through your body as DJs and selectors compete with the newest hits and vintage melodies, igniting dance floors and sparking passions.

Beach Parties and After-Parties: Continue the fun into the night with beach parties, after-parties, and special events held at various locations across Montego Bay. Dance beneath the stars to the irresistible rhythms of reggae and dancehall music, socialize with other attendees, and soak up the exuberant atmosphere of Jamaica's finest music festival.

To summarize, Ocho Rios provides a dynamic tapestry of festivals and events that honor the island's cultural past, musical tradition, and spirit of togetherness and innovation. From jazz concerts to reggae festivities, these local festivals provide immersive experiences that highlight Jamaica's rich cultural traditions while bringing people together through music, dancing, and community.

Chapter 16

PHOTOGRAPHY AND SIGHTSEEING TIPS.

Exploring Ocho Rios has a wealth of beautiful panoramas, cultural diversity, and bright sceneries that are just waiting to be caught via your camera lens. From beautiful beaches to thick jungles, Ocho Rios is a photographer's dream, with countless options for breathtaking pictures and unforgettable photos.

In this chapter, we'll look at the greatest photographic locations, how to capture the spirit of Jamaican culture, and how to conduct polite photography practices.

Top Photography Spots in Ocho Rios

Ocho Rios has a broad range of gorgeous landscapes, historical sites, and cultural attractions that allow photography enthusiasts to capture the beauty and soul of Jamaica. Here are some of the top picture places in Ocho Rios:

Dunn's River Falls: One of Jamaica's most famous natural marvels, Dunn's River Falls provides breathtaking photo possibilities with its tumbling waterfalls, rich greenery, and crystalline pools. Capture the magnificence of the falls from numerous viewing points along the rising stairs, or dive into the cold waters for new views.

Mystic Mountain: Take a picturesque tour into Mystic Mountain's dense rainforest canopy, where you can see panoramic views of Ocho Rios' shoreline and green surroundings. Take the Sky Explorer chairlift to the hilltop for panoramic views, or soar through the trees on a thrilling zipline adventure.

Mahogany Beach: Located along Ocho Rios' coastline, Mahogany Beach features pure white beaches, blue seas, and swaying palm trees that are great for photographing postcard-perfect beach vistas. Frame your photographs against the Caribbean Sea, snap intimate moments with beachgoers, or bask in the golden glow of a Jamaican sunset.

Shaw Park Gardens: Discover the botanical delights of Shaw Park Gardens, where vibrant blossoms, exotic plants, and serene water features give limitless inspiration for photographers. Stroll through verdant pathways, take close-up photos of tropical flowers, and enjoy the tranquility of this hidden treasure in Ocho Rios.

Ocho Rios Craft Market: Immerse yourself in Jamaican culture by capturing the brilliant colors, busy ambiance, and distinctive workmanship of the Ocho Rios Craft Market. Photograph artists at work, explore handcrafted products, and mingle with people to get a true sense of Jamaican culture.

Embracing The Essence of Jamaican Culture

Jamaican culture is a tapestry of vivid colors, rich customs, and genuine hospitality that begs to be caught on camera. To fully capture the essence of Jamaican culture in your images, explore the following suggestions:

Connect with Locals: To capture true moments and genuine relationships, immerse yourself in the fabric of Jamaican life. Strike up a discussion, get permission before shooting photos, and respect the cultural traditions and customs of the people you visit.

Document Cultural festivities: Attend local festivals, parades, and festivities to capture the vibrant and diverse Jamaican culture. From vibrant street performances to ancient dance rites, these events provide unique chances to capture the passion and energy of the island's cultural history.

Pay attention to the intricacies that distinguish Jamaican culture, such as exquisite handicrafts, bright street art, and architectural quirks. Capture the feel of woven fabrics, the brilliant colors of painted murals, and the detailed designs of traditional artwork to create a visual tale about Jamaican identity and creativity.

Embrace Reggae Rhythms: Reggae music is central to Jamaican culture, inspiring generations with its captivating rhythms and passionate songs. Capture the essence of reggae with intimate photographs of singers, vivid concert scenes, and spontaneous dance parties that celebrate music as a worldwide language.

Celebrate Diversity: Jamaica is a melting pot of cultures, faiths, and customs, all of which add to the vivid fabric of island life. Embrace Jamaican society's variety by capturing moments of harmony, friendliness, and mutual respect that cross cultural borders and celebrate everyone's shared humanity.

Photo Etiquette and Respectful Practices

While photographing the beauty of Ocho Rios, it is essential to follow photographic etiquette and demonstrate respect for the nature, culture, and people you encounter. Here are some important rules to make your photographic experience enjoyable and considerate:

Obtain Consent: Always request permission before photographing someone, especially in close-up portraits or intimate circumstances. Approach individuals with dignity, explain your goals, and accept their decision if they refuse to be photographed. Respect cultural sensitivity when photographing, particularly in holy or private locations.

Respect holy places and Ceremonies: Use caution while shooting religious or holy places, ceremonies, or rituals. Follow any signs or photographic rules, and avoid intruding on private moments or disturbing spiritual rituals. Maintain a polite distance and get permission when necessary.

Be Aware of Your Environment: Pay attention to your surroundings and make sure your photographic activities do not upset wildlife, harm natural ecosystems, or restrict routes. Reduce your environmental effect by practicing responsible tourism and following the Leave No Trace principles.

Cultural Sensitivity: Learn about the local norms, traditions, and taboos surrounding photography in Ocho Rios. Respect cultural traditions for modesty, privacy, and personal space, particularly while photography in communities or at cultural events. Avoid using your photographs to perpetuate stereotypes or misrepresentations.

Consider the Impact of Your Presence: Be mindful of how your presence and photographic activities may impact the local community and environment. Avoid overcrowding or disturbing daily life in pursuit of images, and put the well-being and comfort of others around you first. Engage with locals in a courteous manner and explore chances for cultural exchange and understanding.

Share Stories with Integrity: Use your photographs to communicate honest stories about the variety, resilience, and beauty of Ocho Rios and its residents. Strive to capture actual events and storylines that challenge preconceptions, encourage empathy, and promote cross-cultural understanding. Respect your people' dignity and autonomy by expressing them accurately and ethically.

Practice Responsible Social Media posting: When posting photos on social media, use judgment and sensitivity. Obtain consent from the people in your pictures, and avoid publishing images that are intrusive, rude, or culturally inappropriate. Captions can help to offer context and emphasize the value of the places and people in your images.

Make a Positive influence: As a responsible photographer, strive to have a positive influence on the communities and surroundings you visit. Support local businesses, artists, and projects that encourage eco-tourism and cultural preservation. Leave a legacy of respect, admiration, and mutual understanding wherever your photographic adventure takes you.

By following these photographic etiquette principles and behaving respectfully, you may make significant relationships, record real moments, and help to preserve and appreciate Ocho Rios' cultural and natural history through your photos.

Chapter 17

SAFETY AND TRAVEL TIPS.

Providing a safe and pleasurable travel experience in Ocho Rios requires early preparation, understanding of possible dangers, and adherence to responsible travel standards.

This chapter covers everything from health and safety considerations to emergency contacts and responsible conduct, allowing guests to explore Ocho Rios with confidence and peace of mind.

Health and Safety Precautions.

Prioritizing health and safety is critical whether visiting Ocho Rios or any other place. Travelers can reduce dangers and fully enjoy their vacation by taking proactive precautions and following recommended instructions. Here are some important health and safety considerations to consider:

Stay Hydrated: Jamaica's tropical environment may be hot and humid, resulting in dehydration. Carry a reusable water bottle and stay hydrated, especially while participating in outdoor activities or spending time in the sun.

Mosquito Protection: Mosquito-borne diseases like dengue fever and the Zika virus are a major issue in tropical areas. To lessen the risk of bites, apply DEET-based insect repellent, wear long-sleeved clothes, and sleep beneath mosquito nets.

Sun Protection: Use high-SPF sunscreen on a daily basis, especially if you spend time outside. To avoid sunburn and heat sickness, wear a wide-brimmed hat, sunglasses, and lightweight clothes.

Food and Water Safety: Be cautious while eating and drinking from street sellers or unknown institutions. To reduce the danger of foodborne disease, drink bottled water and eat fresh, hot meals.

Medical Precautions: Before visiting, consult with a healthcare provider to confirm you are current on standard vaccinations and any special vaccines suggested for Jamaica. Consider obtaining travel insurance to protect against unforeseen medical expenditures or emergencies.

COVID-19 Protocols: Stay current on COVID-19 policies and norms imposed by local governments and enterprises. To help prevent the virus from spreading, practice physical distance, use face masks in crowded or confined areas, and follow cleanliness practices.

Emergency Contacts and Services.

Travelers visiting Ocho Rios must be prepared to deal with emergencies. Familiarize oneself with the emergency contacts and services in the region to ensure fast aid if necessary. Here are some important emergency contacts to have handy:

Emergency Services: In the event of an emergency, phone 119 to contact local police, fire, or medical services. To help expedite assistance, provide detailed facts about the nature of the incident and your location.

Hospital and Medical Facilities: Locate the closest hospitals, clinics, and medical facilities in Ocho Rios. The Hospital Ocho Rios and the Ocho Rios Health Centre are primary healthcare facilities that can manage medical crises and provide critical services to guests.

Embassy or Consulate: Look for the contact details for your country's embassy or consulate in Jamaica. Embassy staff can help with passport replacement, legal concerns, and emergency evacuation assistance if necessary.

Travel Insurance Provider: Keep a copy of your travel insurance policy and your insurance provider's contact details on hand. In the event of a medical emergency, call your insurance carrier to begin the claims procedure and get advice on how to obtain healthcare services.

Communicate openly with your trip providers, guides, and accommodations. They can offer help, information, and support in the event of an emergency or unanticipated scenario during your stay in Ocho Rios.

Responsible Travel Practices

Responsible travel entails respecting local traditions, reducing environmental damage, and positively contributing to the communities you visit. By adopting responsible travel behaviors, tourists may promote sustainable tourism and leave a good legacy. Here are the fundamental guidelines of responsible travel to follow in Ocho Rios.

Cultural Respect: Honor the practices, traditions, and beliefs of the local community. Seek for chances for cultural interaction, acquire some basic words in the local language, and interact with natives with humility and curiosity.

Environmental Stewardship: Reduce your environmental impact by adopting eco-friendly practices such as trash reduction, water and energy conservation, and supporting businesses that prioritize sustainability programs.

Support Local Communities: Shop at locally owned companies, craftsmen, and venues to directly benefit the local economy. Buy souvenirs and handicrafts from craftsmen, eat at family-run eateries, and take part in community-based excursions and activities.

Leave No Trace: Respect natural and cultural areas by disposing of garbage correctly and refraining from littering. Follow established paths, protect wildlife habitats, and do not remove or disrupt natural objects or resources.

Responsible Wildlife Interaction: When participating in wildlife encounters or nature-based activities, put animal welfare and conservation first. Choose ethical operators that follow safe wildlife watching methods and avoid participating in activities that exploit or injure animals for entertainment.

Encourage inclusion and Equity: Value diversity, encourage inclusion, and respect the rights and dignity of all people, regardless of background or identity. Encourage genuine connections and work to build inclusive environments in which everyone feels welcome and appreciated.

By taking health and safety precautions, becoming acquainted with emergency contacts, and practicing responsible travel behavior, you can have a safe, enriching, and rewarding experience in Ocho Rios while also contributing to the well-being of local communities and the preservation of Jamaica's natural and cultural heritage.

Chapter 18

BUDGET-FRIENDLY TRAVEL TIPS.

A trip to Ocho Rios does not have to be expensive. With careful preparation, clever budgeting, and a little imagination, you can enjoy everything this dynamic destination has to offer without breaking the bank.

In this chapter, we'll look at practical advice and tactics for saving money, finding reasonable food alternatives, and participating in free or low-cost activities in Ocho Rios.

Ways to Save Money in Ocho Rios.

Exploring Ocho Rios on a budget necessitates careful budgeting and clever preparation. Here are some practical techniques to stretch your dollar and maximize your vacation budget:

Travel Off-Peak: Visit Ocho Rios during the shoulder season or off-peak months, when hotel costs and visitor throngs are lower. Determine the optimal time to go based on seasonal trends and take advantage of lower prices and special offers.

Choose Budget-Friendly Accommodations: Instead of high-end resorts, stay in guesthouses, hostels, or vacation rentals. Look for savings and discounts on booking sites, and seek alternate hotel alternatives that provide value without losing comfort or convenience.

Use Public Transportation: To move about Ocho Rios and visit surrounding sites, take public buses, shared taxis (route taxis), or minibuses (coasters). Public transportation is inexpensive and provides an opportunity to explore local culture directly.

Cook Your Own Meals: Save money on dining out by making your own meals or snacks with locally obtained goods from markets or grocery stores. Book lodgings with kitchens to prepare simple meals, pack picnic lunches for day travels, and enjoy low-cost eating alternatives without sacrificing flavor.

Look for Free Attractions: Take advantage of free or low-cost attractions and activities in Ocho Rios, including as public beaches, botanical gardens, and beautiful overlooks. Look into local festivals, cultural events, and community meetings that provide meaningful experiences for little or no cost.

Negotiate Prices: Learn the skill of haggling whether buying at markets or participating in guided tours or excursions. Don't be afraid to ask for discounts or inquire about special specials, especially when purchasing souvenirs or arranging activities directly with local sellers.

Pack Light and Smart: To avoid additional baggage fees and other costs, pack light and smart. Bring basic things and adaptable attire appropriate for the tropical temperature, and consider carrying reusable water bottles and snacks to minimize impulsive purchases while exploring.

Affordable Dining Options

Eating good on a budget in Ocho Rios is definitely possible with a little forethought and effort. Here are some reasonably priced eating alternatives to consider:

Local Eateries and Street Food: Try real Jamaican cuisine at local restaurants, food stalls, and street vendors that serve tasty and reasonably priced meals. Enjoy traditional meals such as jerk chicken, ackee and saltfish, and patties while immersing yourself in the island's gastronomic offerings.

Market Meals: Explore Ocho Rios' lively markets, such as the Ocho Rios Craft Market and the Pineapple Craft Market, for fresh vegetables, spices, and handcrafted snacks. Enjoy affordable meals provided by local vendors, such as fresh fruits, grilled meats, and flavorful savory snacks.

Budget-Friendly Restaurants: Look for restaurants and cafés that cater to budget-conscious tourists, providing inexpensive menu selections without sacrificing taste or quality. Look for daily specials, lunch bargains, and early bird promos to get tasty meals at a reduced price.

Cook Your Own Meals: Take use of your accommodation's self-catering facilities to create meals using locally sourced foods. Visit supermarkets, grocery shops, or farmers' markets to stock up on necessities and prepare easy, low-cost meals that represent Jamaican cuisine.

Bring Your Own Snacks: Pack snacks and drinks for day trips and excursions to save money on pricey convenience products. Bring a reusable water bottle, trail mix, fruits, and energy bars to remain hydrated and energized while visiting Ocho Rios on a budget.

Free or Low-cost Activities

Discovering Ocho Rios on a budget does not imply missing out on unforgettable experiences. There are various free and low-cost activities that allow you to experience Jamaica's beauty, culture, and spirit without breaking the bank. Here are some cost-effective choices to consider:

Beach Days: Relax in the sun and enjoy the warm Caribbean waves at Ocho Rios' public beaches. Turtle and Mahogany Beach have immaculate sands and crystal-clear seas ideal for swimming, sunbathing, and beach picnics. Bring a towel, sunscreen, and plenty of water for a day of rest and renewal.

Wildlife Walks and Hiking Trails: Put on your hiking boots and experience Ocho Rios' beautiful hiking trails and wildlife reserves. Trek through beautiful woods, find secret waterfalls, and marvel at panoramic views of the coastline. Popular routes include the Dunn's River Falls Trail and the Konoko Falls Nature Trail, which provide chances for adventure and discovery in Jamaica's natural splendor.

Botanical Gardens and Parks: Take a leisurely stroll through Ocho Rios' botanical gardens and parks, where you can see exotic vegetation, peaceful water features, and beautifully groomed landscapes. Shaw Park Gardens and Turtle River Park are popular locations for nature enthusiasts, providing peaceful surroundings for leisure and photography.

Cultural Events and Festivals: Get involved in Ocho Rios' thriving cultural scene by attending free or low-cost events and festivals honoring Jamaican music, dance, and craftsmanship. Keep a look out for live performances, street festivals, and cultural festivities that highlight the island's diverse history and vibrant cultural traditions.

Historical Sites and Landmarks: Visit historical sites and landmarks in Ocho Rios to learn about Jamaica's history and tradition. Discover the remnants of Fort Dundas, learn about Jamaica's indigenous Taino culture at the Columbus Park Museum, or take a stroll around the old town center to enjoy colonial architecture and colorful street paintings.

Local Markets & artisan festivals: Discover the bright sights, sounds, and flavors of Jamaica by visiting Ocho Rios' busy markets and artisan festivals. Browse stalls offering handcrafted goods, souvenirs, and local artwork at the Ocho Rios Craft Market or the Pineapple Craft Market, where you may bargain for unique finds and support local entrepreneurs.

Beach Cleanups and Conservation Activities: Help your community and the environment by taking part in beach cleanups and conservation activities conducted by local organizations and volunteer groups. Join like-minded visitors and residents in protecting Ocho Rios' pristine shoreline and marine ecosystems while having a beneficial influence on the environment.

Community Workshops and Cultural Experiences: Connect with the local community through workshops, cultural exchanges, and immersive experiences that provide insight into Jamaican culture and traditions. Learn to salsa dance or prepare traditional Jamaican delicacies, join drum circles, or attend storytelling sessions that highlight the island's diverse culture and traditions.

Self-Guided Walking Tours: Take self-guided walking tours of Ocho Rios' neighborhoods, historic places, and picturesque features to explore the city at your own leisure. Pick up a map at the tourist information center or download a digital guide to discover hidden jewels, architectural marvels, and local hotspots off the main road.

Taking advantage of these free and low-cost activities allows you to create amazing memories and meaningful experiences in Ocho Rios without exceeding your trip budget.

Chapter 19

CULTURAL ETIQUETTE AND CUSTOMS.

Understanding and respecting the cultural norms and practices of Ocho Rios and Jamaica in general is critical for meaningful interactions and immersion experiences.

In this chapter, we'll look at the nuances of Jamaican greetings, the relevance of Rastafarian culture, and the value of honoring local traditions and customs in order to negotiate cultural encounters with grace and compassion.

Jamaican Greetings And Social Norms.

Greetings are important in Jamaican culture because they show the country's deep-rooted warmth, friendliness, and respect for others. Understanding Jamaican greetings and social conventions may improve your interactions and develop positive relationships with the people. Keep in mind the following standard greetings and social norms:

Warmth and Friendliness: Jamaicans are recognized for their warm and friendly disposition, and they frequently greet one another with smiles, handshakes, and professions of goodwill. Accept this openness and conduct encounters with true warmth and honesty.

Use of Informal Language: Jamaican English is distinguished by its vibrant slang, idioms, and casual conversational manner. Don't be shocked if locals use informal language or idioms like "yah man" (yeah, of course) or "big up" (greetings or respect) in casual conversation.

Respect for seniors: In Jamaican society, seniors are revered and treated with deference. Use titles like "Miss" or "Mister" followed by the person's last name to show respect, especially when meeting seniors for the first time.

Handshakes and Physical Contact: In Jamaica, handshakes are commonly exchanged, generally accompanied by a tight grasp and direct eye contact. Physical contact and affectionate gestures, such as hugs or cheek kisses, are typical ways to communicate friendship and connection.

Punctuality and Flexibility: While punctuality is respected in Jamaican society, there is also a laid-back attitude toward time known as "island time." Expect events and meetings to start later than planned, and exercise patience and flexibility when plans inevitably alter.

Respect for Personal Space: Jamaicans cherish personal space and may like to maintain a comfortable distance during talks and encounters. Respect people's boundaries and avoid approaching or violating their personal space, particularly with strangers or acquaintances.

Politeness and civility: In Jamaican culture, politeness and civility are highly prized, and it is necessary to always show respect and regard for others. Use "please," "thank you," and "excuse me" regularly in talks, and always express appreciation for hospitality or help.

By adopting Jamaican greetings and social standards, you may cultivate positive relationships, establish rapport, and negotiate cultural encounters with confidence and respect.

Understanding Rastafari Culture

Rastafarian culture is an essential aspect of Jamaican identity, embracing spiritual beliefs, cultural rituals, and a distinct way of life steeped in African origin and resistance against oppression. Understanding the ideals and symbols of Rastafarian culture will improve your visit to Jamaica and deepen your understanding for the country's unique cultural tapestry. Here are crucial factors to consider:

Spiritual Beliefs: Rastafarianism is a spiritual movement that arose in Jamaica in the early twentieth century, inspired by Marcus Garvey's teachings and the Ethiopian monarch Haile Selassie I, whom Rastafarians see as the messiah or "Jah."

Dreadlocks & Appearance: Dreadlocks are a distinguishing aspect of Rastafarian culture, representing a return to African origins, spiritual consciousness, and defiance of conventional standards. Respect people's decision to wear dreadlocks and avoid touching or commenting on their hair without permission.

Ital Lifestyle: Rastafarians follow a "Ital" lifestyle, which includes eating natural, unprocessed foods and committing to holistic health and wellness. When eating with Rastafarians, respect their dietary choices and practices, and avoid giving meat or alcohol, as these may contradict with their beliefs.

Language and Music: Rastafarian culture has affected Jamaican language, music, and art, with reggae music serving as an effective vehicle for transmitting Rastafarian ideas of unity, freedom, and social justice. Examine the words and rhythms of reggae music to acquire insight into Rastafarian ideology and worldview.

Symbols and hues: Rastafarian culture is rich in symbolism, with hues like red, gold, and green signifying the Ethiopian flag and the three Rastafarian principles: love, unity, and righteousness. Respect Rastafarian symbols and artifacts, like the Lion of Judah and the Rasta flag, as holy manifestations of religion and identity.

Respect and Empathy: Enter into talks about Rastafarian culture with respect, empathy, and a willingness to learn. Avoid cultural appropriation or monetization of Rastafarian symbols and traditions, and instead seek out chances for genuine discourse and cultural exchange with Rastafarians.

Recognizing and respecting Rastafarian culture's values and practices allows you to form meaningful connections, enhance cultural understanding, and appreciate Jamaica's rich legacy and variety.

Respect of Local Traditions and Customs

Respecting local traditions and practices is not simply an issue of cultural sensitivity; it is also an essential component of responsible and fulfilling travel. Travelers may form true relationships and acquire deeper insights into Jamaica's unique cultural tapestry by honoring the customs, rituals, and beliefs of the local population in Ocho Rios and around the country. Here are some significant traditions and conventions to follow:

Religious Observances: Jamaica is known for its religious variety, with Christianity being the major faith. Respect religious observances, customs, and practices, and remember to attend church services or religious rituals with regard and respect.

Festivities & Festivals: Jamaicans are recognized for their festive attitude, and the island organizes a variety of exciting festivals, cultural events, and holiday festivities all year. Accept the chance to take part in local festivals with excitement and an open heart, immersing yourself in the rhythms, customs, and rituals that characterize Jamaican culture.

Family and Community Values: Family is important to Jamaican culture, and strong family and communal solidarity are highly prized. Respect the value of family ties and community solidarity, and be willing to engage with locals through shared meals, meetings, and community activities that promote a sense of belonging and connection.

Creative Expression: Jamaica has a strong legacy of creative expression, ranging from vivid murals and street art to complex handicrafts and sculptures. Show your support for local artisans and craftsmen by purchasing handcrafted souvenirs, artwork, and textiles that reflect Jamaica's cultural history and creative energy.

Environmental Stewardship: Jamaica's natural beauty inspires pride and reverence among its people, who have a strong respect for the environment and a dedication to conservation. To protect Jamaica's beautiful landscapes and biodiversity for future generations, adopt eco-friendly behaviors and responsible tourist practices such as reducing trash, saving water and energy, and protecting natural ecosystems.

Cultural Sensitivity: Show cultural sensitivity and understanding in your contacts with locals, appreciating the range of beliefs, customs, and lifestyles that make up Jamaica's cultural mosaic. Approach cultural differences with curiosity, humility, and respect, looking for chances for cross-cultural interchange and discourse to promote mutual understanding and appreciation.

By embracing and respecting the traditions and rituals of the local population in Ocho Rios and Jamaica, visitors may deepen their cultural immersion, form genuine connections, and positively contribute to the preservation and celebration of the island's unique past.

Chapter 20

SUSTAINABLE TOURISM INITIATIVES IN OCHO RIOS.

Sustainable tourism is critical to conserving Ocho Rios' natural beauty, cultural history, and community well-being for future generations.

In this chapter, we look at the creative projects and ethical practices that promote sustainability, environmental protection, and community participation in Ocho Rios.

Environmentally Friendly Accommodations

Choosing eco-friendly hotels is an effective method to reduce your environmental impact while also supporting companies that are dedicated to sustainable practices. Ocho Rios has a variety of eco-friendly accommodation alternatives that promote both environmental responsibility and client comfort. The following are some features of eco-friendly lodgings in Ocho Rios:

Energy Efficiency: Eco-friendly lodgings promote energy efficiency by utilizing renewable energy sources such as solar panels, wind turbines, and energy-saving appliances. To lower power use, seek out lodgings with ENERGY STAR certifications and energy-saving programs like as LED lights and motion sensors.

Water Conservation: In Ocho Rios, where water resources are few and valuable, eco-friendly hotels prioritize water conservation. Choose lodgings with water-saving fixtures, low-flow toilets, and rainwater harvesting systems to reduce water use and encourage sustainable water management practices.

Waste Reduction and Recycling: Sustainable lodgings use waste reduction and recycling initiatives to reduce landfill trash and encourage responsible waste disposal. Look for hotels that include recycling bins, composting facilities, and biodegradable amenities to reduce environmental impact and promote responsible consumption.

Sustainable Design and Construction: Eco-friendly accommodations promote sustainable design and construction methods, such as using eco-friendly building materials, green roofs, and passive heating and cooling systems, to reduce environmental impact and improve energy efficiency. Stay at lodgings that use sustainable construction and green building concepts to promote eco-friendly tourism.

Community Engagement and Social Responsibility: Sustainable lodgings actively connect with local communities and support social responsibility projects that assist inhabitants while also promoting economic empowerment. Choose lodgings that highlight fair labor practices, support local craftsmen and companies, and help fund community development programs including education, healthcare, and infrastructure upgrades.

Certifications and accreditations: Look for eco-friendly lodgings that have been accredited by recognized organizations like Green Globe, EarthCheck, or LEED (Leadership in Energy and Environmental Design) for their dedication to sustainable tourism and environmental stewardship. These certifications ensure that lodgings follow stringent sustainability criteria and are audited and assessed on a regular basis.

Choosing eco-friendly lodgings in Ocho Rios allows guests to reduce their environmental impact, support sustainable tourism projects, and help preserve Jamaica's natural resources and cultural legacy.

Conservation Efforts.

Conservation activities are critical to safeguarding Ocho Rios' unique ecosystems, wildlife habitats, and natural monuments from environmental deterioration and overexploitation. Conservation groups and local stakeholders are working together via collaborative partnerships and community-driven projects to protect Ocho Rios' natural riches for future generations. Here are some conservation activities going on in Ocho Rios:

Marine Conservation: Ocho Rios is home to thriving coral reefs, marine sanctuaries, and protected marine regions rich in biodiversity. Conservation groups like the Caribbean Coastal Area Management Foundation (C-CAM) use education, research, and lobbying to protect and restore coral reefs, prevent marine pollution, and promote sustainable fishing methods.

Forest Protection and Restoration: Ocho Rios is bordered by beautiful rainforests, natural reserves, and protected areas that provide habitat for a broad range of flora and animals. Conservation organizations like the Jamaica Conservation and Development Trust (JCDT) work with government agencies, local communities, and international partners to protect forest ecosystems, combat deforestation, and restore degraded habitats through reforestation and habitat rehabilitation projects.

Animal Conservation: Ocho Rios has a varied range of animal species, including indigenous birds, reptiles, and mammals that rely on healthy ecosystems to survive. The Jamaica Environment Trust (JET) and other organizations use education and outreach initiatives to protect and conserve animal habitats, reduce human-wildlife conflicts, and create awareness about the need of biodiversity conservation.

Environmental Education and Awareness: Environmental education is essential for raising environmental awareness and instilling a feeling of responsibility in both local inhabitants and visitors. Conservation organizations, nature centers, and eco-tourism operators provide educational programs, guided tours, and hands-on activities that involve participants in environmental conservation and sustainability initiatives, allowing them to make informed decisions and take action to protect Ocho Rios' natural heritage.

Sustainable agricultural and Land Management: In Ocho Rios, sustainable agricultural approaches like as organic farming, agroforestry, and permaculture are promoted to reduce environmental impact, protect soil and water resources, and improve food security and resilience in local communities. Organizations such as the Rural Agricultural Development Authority (RADA) help farmers adopt sustainable land management methods and increase agricultural output while maintaining natural ecosystems.

Protected Area Management: Ocho Rios has various protected areas and national parks, including as Dunn's River Falls, Mystic Mountain, and Fern Gully that are maintained and controlled to guarantee sustainable tourism development and environmental preservation. To ensure responsible stewardship and long-term sustainability, protected area management plans prioritize combining conservation goals with visitor enjoyment, infrastructural development, and community engagement.

Supporting conservation activities in Ocho Rios allows visitors to help preserve natural resources, biodiversity, and cultural history while also encouraging sustainable tourism practices and leaving a legacy of environmental care for future generations.

Community Engagement Projects

Community involvement programs are critical for promoting sustainable tourism practices and ensuring that local communities in Ocho Rios benefit from tourism growth. These efforts empower residents, encourage socioeconomic development, and protect cultural heritage. Below are some examples of community participation projects in Ocho Rios:

Skills Training and Capacity Building: Community groups and non-governmental organizations (NGOs) work together to deliver skills training and capacity-building programs to local inhabitants. These projects include vocational training in hospitality, tourism services, craft-making, and sustainable agriculture, giving community residents vital skills and job prospects in the tourism sector.

Cultural Preservation and history Tourism: Community-driven projects aim to preserve and promote Ocho Rios' diverse cultural history through heritage tourism initiatives. Local artists, performers, and cultural practitioners interact with guests via guided tours, seminars, and cultural experiences that emphasize Jamaican customs, music, dance, and food, conserving cultural authenticity while providing money to community residents.

Community-Based Tourism Enterprises: Community-based tourism businesses allow local communities to participate in tourist activities and directly profit from visitor spending. These programs include community-led homestays, cultural tours, and eco-tourism experiences that provide authentic insights into Jamaican culture and lifestyle while also establishing long-term livelihoods and economic possibilities for communities.

Environmental Conservation and Clean-Up Campaigns: Community-led environmental conservation initiatives aim to protect Ocho Rios' natural landscapes, marine habitats, and coastal regions. Residents take part in beach clean-up activities, tree planting projects, and recycling programs to help the environment, create awareness about pollution prevention, and encourage acceptable waste management practices in their town.

Youth Empowerment and Education: Youth empowerment initiatives seek to inspire and educate Ocho Rios' future generation of leaders and entrepreneurs. These projects offer mentorship, educational subsidies, and extracurricular activities that encourage youngsters to achieve academic success, develop leadership abilities, and positively contribute to their communities, instilling pride and resilience in young inhabitants.

Community tourist Committees: These committees facilitate collaboration, dialogue, and decision-making among local stakeholders, tourist providers, and government organizations. These committees advocate for community interests, address tourist development problems, and guarantee that community voices are heard in decision-making processes, therefore fostering openness, accountability, and inclusive governance in the tourism industry.

Cultural Festivals and Events: Community-organized cultural festivals and events highlight Ocho Rios' rich tradition and creative talent while also encouraging community cohesiveness and economic growth. Events like the Ocho Rios Jazz Festival, Bob Marley Birthday Celebration, and Reggae Sumfest draw people from all over the world, boosting local businesses, providing revenue for craftsmen and vendors, and instilling a feeling of pride and cultural identity in the town.

Volunteer Tourism Programs: Volunteer tourism programs allow visitors to participate in meaningful community service initiatives while visiting Ocho Rios. Volunteers support education, healthcare, environmental conservation, and community development initiatives by collaborating with local organizations and community members to address pressing social and environmental challenges, fostering cross-cultural understanding, and positively impacting residents' lives.

By actively participating in community engagement projects, visitors can support sustainable tourism practices, promote social inclusion and economic empowerment, and contribute to the well-being and resilience of Ocho Rios' vibrant communities, ensuring that tourism benefits are distributed equitably among all stakeholders.

Chapter 21

PLANNING SPECIAL EVENTS IN OCHO RIOS

Ocho Rios, with its stunning surroundings, romantic ambiance, and dynamic culture, provides an amazing setting for special events like as destination weddings, honeymoons, and anniversary parties.

In this chapter, we'll look at the particular chances and considerations for creating amazing memories in Ocho Rios.

Destination Weddings.

Ocho Rios embodies romance, making it an ideal location for couples looking for a beautiful environment to exchange vows and celebrate their love. Planning a vacation wedding in Ocho Rios allows couples to make lasting memories against a background of blue seas, beautiful gardens, and gushing waterfalls. Here's all you need to know to organize your perfect wedding in Ocho Rios:

Choosing the Perfect Venue: Ocho Rios has a variety of breathtaking destination wedding sites, ranging from opulent resorts and beachfront villas to botanical gardens and ancient estates. Consider Moon Palace Jamaica, Sandals Ochi Beach Resort, and Turtle River Park for its beautiful beauty, exceptional service, and customizable wedding packages tailored to your specific needs and budget.

Legal procedures and papers: Before you plan your vacation wedding in Ocho Rios, be sure you understand the legal procedures and papers required to marry in Jamaica. Couples must seek a marriage license from the Ministry of Justice and present valid passports, birth certificates, and proof of marital status. It is recommended that you hire a local wedding planner or resort coordinator to help you negotiate the legal procedure and ensure that you follow Jamaican marriage regulations.

Customized Wedding Packages: Many resorts and wedding venues in Ocho Rios provide customisable wedding packages based on your style, tastes, and budget. From modest beach ceremonies and garden receptions to huge ballroom festivities, you may personalize every element of your wedding, including décor, cuisine, entertainment, and photography, to ensure a memorable experience for you and your guests.

Professional Wedding Services: Ocho Rios is home to a brilliant pool of wedding suppliers and experts, including wedding planners, photographers, florists, musicians, and officiants, who specialize in creating memorable moments and seamless experiences for their clients. Collaborate with seasoned wedding specialists who understand your idea and can bring it to life via their creativity, competence, and attention to detail.

Pre-Wedding Activities and Excursions: Maximize your destination wedding experience in Ocho Rios by planning pre-wedding activities and excursions for you and your guests. Ocho Rios has a multitude of activities for leisure, adventure, and discovery, including snorkeling and sunset cruises, zip-lining experiences, and cultural tours, that will leave everyone with unforgettable memories.

Post-Wedding Honeymoon resort: After exchanging vows, relax and celebrate your new life together in a lovely honeymoon resort in Ocho Rios. Enjoy deluxe accommodations, private beach dinners, couples' spa treatments, and sunset strolls down the beachfront while soaking up the enchantment and romance of your first days as a married couple in paradise.

Planning a destination wedding in Ocho Rios allows couples to make cherished memories in a stunning environment surrounded by the beauty and warmth of Jamaican hospitality and culture.

Honeymoon Packages

Ocho Rios entices newlyweds with its breathtaking beauty, private environment, and a variety of romantic events tailored specifically for honeymooners. Whether you desire adventure, leisure, or cultural immersion, Ocho Rios honeymoon packages are designed to take your post-wedding trip to new heights. Here's things you should consider while arranging your honeymoon in Ocho Rios:

Opulent Accommodations: Ocho Rios offers a variety of opulent resorts, boutique hotels, and private villas for honeymooners seeking seclusion, romance, and individual treatment. Consider Jamaica Inn, Couples Tower Isle, and Hermosa Cove for its wonderful facilities, picturesque surroundings, and honeymoon packages that feature extra goodies like champagne upon arrival, couples' massages, and romantic dinners beneath the stars.

 Romantic Experiences and Activities: From candlelit beach dinners and sunset cruises to horseback riding along the coast and waterfall tours, Ocho Rios has a wide range of romantic experiences and activities for honeymooners to enjoy. Explore the natural beauty of Dunn's River Falls, take a catamaran tour to isolated coves, or simply relax on the beautiful beaches while enjoying the warmth of the Caribbean sun and each other's companionship.

Cultural Immersion and Exploration: Learn about Jamaica's unique culture and legacy through cultural excursions and immersive activities that include music, cuisine, and traditions. Visit ancient plantations, local markets, and craft shops, as well as live reggae concerts and dance performances, to connect with Jamaica's essence and make lasting memories.

Adventure and Thrills: For adventurous couples, Ocho Rios has a variety of adrenaline-pumping activities and excursions that guarantee excitement and thrills. Zip-line through the rainforest canopy, take ATV rides across mountainous terrain, or swim and scuba dive to see the colorful marine life that lives under the seas. Whatever your level of adventure, Ocho Rios has limitless options for exploration and discovery.

Spa and Wellness Retreats: During your honeymoon in Ocho Rios, indulge yourself to relaxing spa treatments and wellness retreats that will revive your mind, body, and soul. Couples massages, holistic healing therapies, and yoga sessions set against the backdrop of lush gardens and calm beaches allow you to rest, rejuvenate, and reconnect in a serene and private setting.

Unique Dining Experiences: Immerse your taste buds in the tastes of Jamaica via unique dining experiences that highlight the island's culinary pleasures and gastronomic treasures. Romantic meals on the beach, private wine tastings, and culinary workshops with famous chefs allow you to taste the freshest local ingredients and the spirit of Jamaican cuisine with each bite.

Whether you choose adventure, leisure, or cultural immersion, Ocho Rios has honeymoon packages to suit every couple's needs and tastes, resulting in amazing moments and cherished memories that will last a lifetime.

Anniversary Celebration

Celebrating years of love and togetherness deserves a special celebration, and Ocho Rios is the ideal setting for marking your most treasured anniversaries. Whether it's your first anniversary or a decade, here's how to create a meaningful anniversary party in Ocho Rios.

 Choosing a Romantic Venue: Ocho Rios offers a variety of romantic places perfect for anniversary celebrations. From private beachfront villas to luxury resorts with spectacular views of the Caribbean Sea, select a location that reflects your love story and sets the tone for an unforgettable celebration.

Customize Your Celebration: Make your anniversary celebration reflect your unique path as a couple. Collaborate with event planners and local vendors to tailor every part of your celebration, from flower arrangements and decor to culinary delights and entertainment, so that each detail reflects your love story and shared experiences.

Renewing Your Vows: Renewing your vows is a moving way to reaffirm your devotion to one another. Plan a vow renewal ceremony at a picturesque setting in Ocho Rios, such as a quiet beach, lush garden, or historic home, surrounded by loved ones and the tranquil beauty of the island.

Indulging in Romantic activities: Make your anniversary celebration genuinely unforgettable by engaging in romantic activities designed just for couples. Enjoy a sunset sail along the coast, a private island tour, or couples' spa treatments and intimate meals beneath the stars to create lasting memories.

Capture the Moment: Hire expert photographers and videographers to document your anniversary celebration. Hire a skilled photographer to capture candid moments, breathtaking backgrounds, and emotional feelings, so you can enjoy the beauty of your anniversary celebration for years to come.

Creating Meaningful Traditions: Creating meaningful traditions may give your anniversary celebrations more depth and purpose. Whether it's writing loving letters, revisiting important places, or going on yearly trips, establish rituals that enhance your relationship and commemorate milestones along the way.

Reflecting on Your Journey: During your anniversary celebration, take time to reflect on your couple's journey and celebrate the milestones, struggles, and successes that have helped define your love story. Share memories, express thanks, and reaffirm your dedication to growing your partnership and building a future full of love, laughter, and adventure.

Share the Joy with Loved Ones: Invite close friends and family members to your anniversary celebration, where you may create cherished memories and develop relationships with those who have been a part of your journey. Consider throwing a celebratory dinner or gathering to express your gratitude for the love and support that has enriched your life.

An anniversary party in Ocho Rios is the ideal way to commemorate your love, make lasting memories, and begin a new chapter in your life together, surrounded by the beauty and romance of this tropical paradise.

Chapter 22

CONCLUSIONS AND FINAL TIPS

As your tour through Ocho Rios draws to a conclusion, take a moment to reflect on the wonderful experiences, stunning scenery, and lively culture that made your vacation so memorable.

In this last chapter, we review the highlights of Ocho Rios, provide final suggestions to guests, and share inspiring anecdotes and testimonies that encapsulate the soul of this tropical paradise.

Summary of Ocho Rios Highlights

Throughout your tour of Ocho Rios, you've come across several highlights that reflect the beauty, uniqueness, and charm of this beautiful resort. From flowing waterfalls to gorgeous beaches, here's a list of must-see sites and activities in Ocho Rios:

Dunn's River Falls: Climb the terraced limestone tiers of Dunn's River Falls, one of Jamaica's most famous natural beauties, for an exciting journey. Feel the cool flow of falling water as you walk through the succession of pools and rock formations, surrounded by lush tropical greenery and stunning views.

Mystic Mountain: Take the Sky Explorer chairlift above the treetops to see Mystic Mountain's natural splendor. Mystic Mountain provides thrilling thrills such as zip-lining through the rainforest canopy and bobsledding down the hillside, as well as panoramic views of Ocho Rios and the Caribbean Sea.

Dolphin Cove: Dive into the crystal-clear waters of Dolphin Cove to experience the enchantment of swimming with dolphins, stingrays, and other marine animals. Interact with these clever and lively creatures in their natural environment and make experiences that will last a lifetime.

Ocho Rios Craft Market: Explore the bright booths and artisan stores at the Ocho Rios Craft Market, where you can find unique handcrafted goods, souvenirs, and treasures created by local craftsmen. Engage with merchants, barter for deals, and immerse yourself in the vibrant tapestry of Jamaican culture and creativity.

Rainforest Hiking Trails: Put on your hiking boots and explore the green jungles and lush scenery surrounding Ocho Rios. As you go on an immersive adventure into the heart of

Jamaica's natural splendor, you'll meet twisting pathways, secret waterfalls, and a variety of flora and animals.

Cultural Experiences: Immerse yourself in the rich tapestry of Jamaican culture with gastronomic delights, exuberant music, and passionate dancing. Indulge in traditional Jamaican food, sway to the addictive rhythms of reggae music, and attend colorful celebrations and festivals that capture the essence of the island.

Final Recommendation for Visitors

As you prepare to leave Ocho Rios, here are some last suggestions to improve your experience and make the most of your time in this wonderful destination:

Embrace the Spirit of Adventure: Whether it's finding secret waterfalls, going on adrenaline-pumping adventures, or immersing yourself in local culture, embrace the spirit of adventure and take advantage of every chance to experience Ocho Rios' treasures.

Respect the Environment and Culture: As you tour Ocho Rios, remember to walk softly and be respectful of the island's natural environment and cultural legacy. Practice responsible tourism, contribute to environmental efforts, and interact with local communities with kindness and respect.

Capture Memories Through Photography: Take the time to shoot Ocho Rios' beauty and enchantment. From breathtaking scenery to candid moments of delight and discovery, photography allows you to capture memories and share them with others.

Savor the Flavors of Jamaica: Indulge in the colorful flavors and fragrances of Jamaican cuisine, including jerk chicken, ackee, saltfish, fresh seafood, and tropical fruits. Explore local markets, street food booths, and restaurants to sample traditional meals and experience the island's gastronomic wonders.

Connect with Locals and Share tales: Take the time to meet the kind and hospitable people of Ocho Rios, listen to their tales, and share your own. Engage in meaningful conversations, enjoy cultural exchanges, and form relationships that cross boundaries to improve your adventure.

Inspirational Stories and Testimonials.

As you leave Ocho Rios, we leave you with inspiring anecdotes and testimonials from fellow visitors who have been moved by the beauty of this fascinating destination:

"Ocho Rios exceeded all my expectations! From the moment I set foot on its shores, I was greeted with warm smiles, breathtaking scenery, and a sense of belonging. My heart will always hold a piece of Ocho Rios." - Sarah, a U.S. citizen

"Our destination wedding in Ocho Rios was a dream come true. Surrounded by loved ones and the beauty of Jamaica, we exchanged vows, created memories, and celebrated love in its purest form. Thank you, Ocho Rios, for the most magical day of our lives." - David and Emily, U.K.

"Ocho Rios stole my heart with its natural beauty, vibrant culture, and warm hospitality. From swimming with dolphins to exploring hidden waterfalls, every moment was filled with wonder and adventure. I can't wait to return and create more memories in paradise." - Michael, from Ontario, Canada

As you leave Ocho Rios, may the memories and experiences you've shared stay with you forever, inspiring future adventures and enriching your life. Farewell till we meet again, and may your journey be blessed with joy, exploration, and limitless possibilities.

APPENDIX

USEFUL RESOURCES

These resources, which include emergency contact information, navigational tools, and local terminology, can help you traverse the location with confidence and comfort.

Emergency Contacts:

It is critical that you have emergency contact information throughout your stay in Ocho Rios in case of unanticipated events or crises. Here are some crucial connections to have handy:

Emergency Services

Police: 119.

Ambulance: 110.

Fire Department: 110.

Medical Assistance

Ocho Rios Hospital, +1 (876) 974-2809.

Medical Emergency Hotline: 911.

Tourism Police

Ocho Rios Tourist Police: +1 (876) 974-2533.

Embassies and Consulates

The Embassy of [Your Country] in Jamaica: [Embassy Website].

Consulate General of [Your Country], Kingston: [Consulate Website]

Maps and Navigational Tools.

Maps and navigational aids make it simpler to navigate Ocho Rios and the neighboring areas. Here are some resources to help you navigate your way around.

Google Maps (www.google.com/maps) provides excellent maps, directions, and real-time traffic updates for traversing Ocho Rios and surrounding attractions.

Jamaica Travel Guide Map: www.visitjamaica.com/map - Shows an interactive map of Jamaica, including Ocho Rios, with attractions, lodgings, and places of interest.

Offline Maps: Use applications like Maps.me or HERE WeGo to traverse Ocho Rios when offline or with poor internet access.

Additional Reading and References

Increase your knowledge and comprehension of Ocho Rios by extra reading and research. Here are a few recommended resources:

Lonely Planet Jamaica: www.lonelyplanet.com/jamaica - Provides comprehensive travel guides, recommendations, and insights for discovering Jamaica, especially Ocho Rios.

Fodor's Jamaica Travel Guide (www.fodors.com/jamaica) - Offers thorough travel guides, reviews, and suggestions for planning your trip to Jamaica.

National Geographic Travel - Jamaica: www.nationalgeographic.com/jamaica - Provides articles, images, and travel ideas for discovering Jamaica's natural wonders, culture, and history.

The Ocho Rios Tourism Board's official website is www.visitjamaica.com/ocho-rios, and it provides visitors with information on attractions, events, lodgings, and travel suggestions.

Useful Local Phrases:

Learn some helpful Jamaican words and expressions to immerse yourself in the culture and interact with the people.

"**Wa gwaan?**" - What's going on? (A common greeting)

2. "One Love" - A phrase meaning unity and respect.

"**No problem, mon**" - Everything is okay, no worries.

"**Irie**" - Feeling good or excellent.

"**Ya man**" - Yes, sure, or okay.

"**Mi deh yah**" - I'm here or I'm good.

Use these phrases to interact with the people and enhance your cultural experience in Ocho Rios.

Addresses and Locations for Popular Accommodations

Moon Palace Jamaica

Address: Main Street, Ocho Rios.

Website: www.moonpalace.com/jamaica

Sandals Ochi Beach Resort

Address: North Coast Highway, Ocho Rios.

Website: www.sandals.com/ochi-beach

Jamaica Inn

Address: 1 Old Road Main Street, Ocho Rios.

Website address: www.jamaicainn.com

Couples Tower Isle

Address: Tower Isle, Ocho Rios

Website: www.couples.com/tower-isle.

Hermosa Cove

Address: Pineapple, Ocho Rios

Website address: www.hermosacove.com

Addresses and locations of popular restaurants and cafes.

Miss T's Kitchen

Address: Main Street, Ocho Rios.

Website address: www.misstskitchen.com

Scotchies' Jerk Center

Address: Main Street, Ocho Rios.

Web address: www.scotchiesjerk.com

Evita's Italian Restaurant

Address: Eden Bower Road, Ocho Rios.

Website address: www.evitasjamaica.com

Toscanini Restaurant

Address: Main Street, Ocho Rios.

Website address: www.toscaninijamaica.com

Margaritaville Ocho Rios.

Address: Island Village, Ocho Rios.

Website: www.margaritavillecaribbean.com/ocho-rios

Addresses And Locations Of Popular Bars And Clubs.

Jimmy Buffett's Margaritaville

Address: Island Village, Ocho Rios.

The website is: www.margaritavillecaribbean.com/ocho-rios

The ruins near the Falls

Address: Dunn's River Falls, Ocho Rios.

Website address: www.ruinsatthefalls.com

Amnesia Nightclub

Address: Main Street, Ocho Rios.

Website address: www.amnesiajamaica.com

Oceans 11

Address: Main Street, Ocho Rios.

Web address: www.oceans11jamaica.com

Margarita Ville Ocho Rios

Address: Island Village, Ocho Rios.

Website: www.margaritavillecaribbean.com/ocho-rios

Addresses And Locations Of The Top Attractions

Dunn's River Falls

Address: Dunn's River Falls Park, Ocho Rios.

Web address: www.dunnsriverfallsja.com

Mystic Mountain

Address: Rainforest Adventures in Ocho Rios

Website: www.rainforestadventures.com/mystic-mountain

Dolphin Cove

Address: Dolphin Cove, Ocho Rios

Web address: www.dolphincoveja.com

Blue Hole

Address: Island Gully Falls, Ocho Rios.

Web address: www.blueholejamaica.com

Konoko Falls

Address: Shaw Park Gardens, Ocho Rios

Website address: www.konokofalls.com

Map of Ocho Rios, Jamaica

https://maps.app.goo.gl/eedewe5sRTDrVCw47

SCAN IMAGE / QR CODE WITH YOUR PHONE

TO GET THE LOCATIONS IN REAL TIME

Map of Restaurants

https://maps.app.goo.gl/yeUPKQVZmEzbYMLy9

SCAN IMAGE / QR CODE WITH YOUR PHONE

TO GET THE LOCATIONS IN REAL TIME

Map of Things to Do in Ocho Rios

https://maps.app.goo.gl/w7Tara1RzEZv7Bsg8

SCAN IMAGE / QR CODE WITH YOUR PHONE

TO GET THE LOCATIONS IN REAL TIME

Map of Museums

https://maps.app.goo.gl/sPBEs3P4zLCVdtN48

SCAN IMAGE / QR CODE WITH YOUR PHONE

TO GET THE LOCATIONS IN REAL TIME

44 55
0345 301 4455
07856 913980 (oon.)

Printed in Dunstable, United Kingdom